ISEE Upper Level Practice Tests

Contents

How To Use This Book

The tests in this book will give you an idea of the types of questions you will see, the concepts that are being tested, and the format and timing of the Upper Level ISEE. You will also get a sense of how the scoring works – one point is given for correct answers and nothing is subtracted for incorrect answers.

Try to work through the test in "real conditions" to get a sense of what it feels like to take a test of this length, which may be longer than what you are used to. Be sure to time yourself on each section and stop when the time is up, just like you will have to on test day.

The following chart lays out the general timing of the test:

Section	Time
Verbal Reasoning – 40 questions	20 minutes
Quantitative Reasoning – 37 questions	35 minutes
--- Five-minute break ---	
Reading Comprehension – 36 questions	35 minutes
Mathematics Achievement – 47 questions	40 minutes
--- Five-minute break ---	
Essay	30 minutes

After you complete Practice Test 1, check all of your answers. Figure out WHY you missed the questions that you answered incorrectly. Then, think about what you would do differently BEFORE you start Practice Test 2.

Answer Sheets

The following pages contain answer sheets for each of the two practice tests.

Practice Test 1

Section 1: Verbal Reasoning

1	(A) (B) (C) (D)	15	(A) (B) (C) (D)	29	(A) (B) (C) (D)
2	(A) (B) (C) (D)	16	(A) (B) (C) (D)	30	(A) (B) (C) (D)
3	(A) (B) (C) (D)	17	(A) (B) (C) (D)	31	(A) (B) (C) (D)
4	(A) (B) (C) (D)	18	(A) (B) (C) (D)	32	(A) (B) (C) (D)
5	(A) (B) (C) (D)	19	(A) (B) (C) (D)	33	(A) (B) (C) (D)
6	(A) (B) (C) (D)	20	(A) (B) (C) (D)	34	(A) (B) (C) (D)
7	(A) (B) (C) (D)	21	(A) (B) (C) (D)	35	(A) (B) (C) (D)
8	(A) (B) (C) (D)	22	(A) (B) (C) (D)	36	(A) (B) (C) (D)
9	(A) (B) (C) (D)	23	(A) (B) (C) (D)	37	(A) (B) (C) (D)
10	(A) (B) (C) (D)	24	(A) (B) (C) (D)	38	(A) (B) (C) (D)
11	(A) (B) (C) (D)	25	(A) (B) (C) (D)	39	(A) (B) (C) (D)
12	(A) (B) (C) (D)	26	(A) (B) (C) (D)	40	(A) (B) (C) (D)
13	(A) (B) (C) (D)	27	(A) (B) (C) (D)		
14	(A) (B) (C) (D)	28	(A) (B) (C) (D)		

Section 2: Quantitative Reasoning

1	(A) (B) (C) (D)	14	(A) (B) (C) (D)	27	(A) (B) (C) (D)
2	(A) (B) (C) (D)	15	(A) (B) (C) (D)	28	(A) (B) (C) (D)
3	(A) (B) (C) (D)	16	(A) (B) (C) (D)	29	(A) (B) (C) (D)
4	(A) (B) (C) (D)	17	(A) (B) (C) (D)	30	(A) (B) (C) (D)
5	(A) (B) (C) (D)	18	(A) (B) (C) (D)	31	(A) (B) (C) (D)
6	(A) (B) (C) (D)	19	(A) (B) (C) (D)	32	(A) (B) (C) (D)
7	(A) (B) (C) (D)	20	(A) (B) (C) (D)	33	(A) (B) (C) (D)
8	(A) (B) (C) (D)	21	(A) (B) (C) (D)	34	(A) (B) (C) (D)
9	(A) (B) (C) (D)	22	(A) (B) (C) (D)	35	(A) (B) (C) (D)
10	(A) (B) (C) (D)	23	(A) (B) (C) (D)	36	(A) (B) (C) (D)
11	(A) (B) (C) (D)	24	(A) (B) (C) (D)	37	(A) (B) (C) (D)
12	(A) (B) (C) (D)	25	(A) (B) (C) (D)		
13	(A) (B) (C) (D)	26	(A) (B) (C) (D)		

Section 3: Reading Comprehension

1	(A) (B) (C) (D)	13	(A) (B) (C) (D)	25	(A) (B) (C) (D)
2	(A) (B) (C) (D)	14	(A) (B) (C) (D)	26	(A) (B) (C) (D)
3	(A) (B) (C) (D)	15	(A) (B) (C) (D)	27	(A) (B) (C) (D)
4	(A) (B) (C) (D)	16	(A) (B) (C) (D)	28	(A) (B) (C) (D)
5	(A) (B) (C) (D)	17	(A) (B) (C) (D)	29	(A) (B) (C) (D)
6	(A) (B) (C) (D)	18	(A) (B) (C) (D)	30	(A) (B) (C) (D)
7	(A) (B) (C) (D)	19	(A) (B) (C) (D)	31	(A) (B) (C) (D)
8	(A) (B) (C) (D)	20	(A) (B) (C) (D)	32	(A) (B) (C) (D)
9	(A) (B) (C) (D)	21	(A) (B) (C) (D)	33	(A) (B) (C) (D)
10	(A) (B) (C) (D)	22	(A) (B) (C) (D)	34	(A) (B) (C) (D)
11	(A) (B) (C) (D)	23	(A) (B) (C) (D)	35	(A) (B) (C) (D)
12	(A) (B) (C) (D)	24	(A) (B) (C) (D)	36	(A) (B) (C) (D)

Section 4: Mathematics Achievement

1	(A) (B) (C) (D)	17	(A) (B) (C) (D)	33	(A) (B) (C) (D)
2	(A) (B) (C) (D)	18	(A) (B) (C) (D)	34	(A) (B) (C) (D)
3	(A) (B) (C) (D)	19	(A) (B) (C) (D)	35	(A) (B) (C) (D)
4	(A) (B) (C) (D)	20	(A) (B) (C) (D)	36	(A) (B) (C) (D)
5	(A) (B) (C) (D)	21	(A) (B) (C) (D)	37	(A) (B) (C) (D)
6	(A) (B) (C) (D)	22	(A) (B) (C) (D)	38	(A) (B) (C) (D)
7	(A) (B) (C) (D)	23	(A) (B) (C) (D)	39	(A) (B) (C) (D)
8	(A) (B) (C) (D)	24	(A) (B) (C) (D)	40	(A) (B) (C) (D)
9	(A) (B) (C) (D)	25	(A) (B) (C) (D)	41	(A) (B) (C) (D)
10	(A) (B) (C) (D)	26	(A) (B) (C) (D)	42	(A) (B) (C) (D)
11	(A) (B) (C) (D)	27	(A) (B) (C) (D)	43	(A) (B) (C) (D)
12	(A) (B) (C) (D)	28	(A) (B) (C) (D)	44	(A) (B) (C) (D)
13	(A) (B) (C) (D)	29	(A) (B) (C) (D)	45	(A) (B) (C) (D)
14	(A) (B) (C) (D)	30	(A) (B) (C) (D)	46	(A) (B) (C) (D)
15	(A) (B) (C) (D)	31	(A) (B) (C) (D)	47	(A) (B) (C) (D)
16	(A) (B) (C) (D)	32	(A) (B) (C) (D)		

Student Name: _____ Grade Applying For: _____
Write in blue or black pen for this essay.

Write your essay topic below

_____
_____
_____

Write your essay below and on the next page

_____
_____
_____
_____
_____
_____
_____
_____
_____
_____
_____
_____
_____
_____
_____
_____
_____
_____
_____
_____
_____
_____
_____
_____

Practice Test 2

Section 1: Verbal Reasoning

1	(A) (B) (C) (D)	15	(A) (B) (C) (D)	29	(A) (B) (C) (D)
2	(A) (B) (C) (D)	16	(A) (B) (C) (D)	30	(A) (B) (C) (D)
3	(A) (B) (C) (D)	17	(A) (B) (C) (D)	31	(A) (B) (C) (D)
4	(A) (B) (C) (D)	18	(A) (B) (C) (D)	32	(A) (B) (C) (D)
5	(A) (B) (C) (D)	19	(A) (B) (C) (D)	33	(A) (B) (C) (D)
6	(A) (B) (C) (D)	20	(A) (B) (C) (D)	34	(A) (B) (C) (D)
7	(A) (B) (C) (D)	21	(A) (B) (C) (D)	35	(A) (B) (C) (D)
8	(A) (B) (C) (D)	22	(A) (B) (C) (D)	36	(A) (B) (C) (D)
9	(A) (B) (C) (D)	23	(A) (B) (C) (D)	37	(A) (B) (C) (D)
10	(A) (B) (C) (D)	24	(A) (B) (C) (D)	38	(A) (B) (C) (D)
11	(A) (B) (C) (D)	25	(A) (B) (C) (D)	39	(A) (B) (C) (D)
12	(A) (B) (C) (D)	26	(A) (B) (C) (D)	40	(A) (B) (C) (D)
13	(A) (B) (C) (D)	27	(A) (B) (C) (D)		
14	(A) (B) (C) (D)	28	(A) (B) (C) (D)		

Section 2: Quantitative Reasoning

1	(A) (B) (C) (D)	14	(A) (B) (C) (D)	27	(A) (B) (C) (D)
2	(A) (B) (C) (D)	15	(A) (B) (C) (D)	28	(A) (B) (C) (D)
3	(A) (B) (C) (D)	16	(A) (B) (C) (D)	29	(A) (B) (C) (D)
4	(A) (B) (C) (D)	17	(A) (B) (C) (D)	30	(A) (B) (C) (D)
5	(A) (B) (C) (D)	18	(A) (B) (C) (D)	31	(A) (B) (C) (D)
6	(A) (B) (C) (D)	19	(A) (B) (C) (D)	32	(A) (B) (C) (D)
7	(A) (B) (C) (D)	20	(A) (B) (C) (D)	33	(A) (B) (C) (D)
8	(A) (B) (C) (D)	21	(A) (B) (C) (D)	34	(A) (B) (C) (D)
9	(A) (B) (C) (D)	22	(A) (B) (C) (D)	35	(A) (B) (C) (D)
10	(A) (B) (C) (D)	23	(A) (B) (C) (D)	36	(A) (B) (C) (D)
11	(A) (B) (C) (D)	24	(A) (B) (C) (D)	37	(A) (B) (C) (D)
12	(A) (B) (C) (D)	25	(A) (B) (C) (D)		
13	(A) (B) (C) (D)	26	(A) (B) (C) (D)		

Section 3: Reading Comprehension

1	(A) (B) (C) (D)	13	(A) (B) (C) (D)	25	(A) (B) (C) (D)
2	(A) (B) (C) (D)	14	(A) (B) (C) (D)	26	(A) (B) (C) (D)
3	(A) (B) (C) (D)	15	(A) (B) (C) (D)	27	(A) (B) (C) (D)
4	(A) (B) (C) (D)	16	(A) (B) (C) (D)	28	(A) (B) (C) (D)
5	(A) (B) (C) (D)	17	(A) (B) (C) (D)	29	(A) (B) (C) (D)
6	(A) (B) (C) (D)	18	(A) (B) (C) (D)	30	(A) (B) (C) (D)
7	(A) (B) (C) (D)	19	(A) (B) (C) (D)	31	(A) (B) (C) (D)
8	(A) (B) (C) (D)	20	(A) (B) (C) (D)	32	(A) (B) (C) (D)
9	(A) (B) (C) (D)	21	(A) (B) (C) (D)	33	(A) (B) (C) (D)
10	(A) (B) (C) (D)	22	(A) (B) (C) (D)	34	(A) (B) (C) (D)
11	(A) (B) (C) (D)	23	(A) (B) (C) (D)	35	(A) (B) (C) (D)
12	(A) (B) (C) (D)	24	(A) (B) (C) (D)	36	(A) (B) (C) (D)

Section 4: Mathematics Achievement

1	(A) (B) (C) (D)	17	(A) (B) (C) (D)	33	(A) (B) (C) (D)
2	(A) (B) (C) (D)	18	(A) (B) (C) (D)	34	(A) (B) (C) (D)
3	(A) (B) (C) (D)	19	(A) (B) (C) (D)	35	(A) (B) (C) (D)
4	(A) (B) (C) (D)	20	(A) (B) (C) (D)	36	(A) (B) (C) (D)
5	(A) (B) (C) (D)	21	(A) (B) (C) (D)	37	(A) (B) (C) (D)
6	(A) (B) (C) (D)	22	(A) (B) (C) (D)	38	(A) (B) (C) (D)
7	(A) (B) (C) (D)	23	(A) (B) (C) (D)	39	(A) (B) (C) (D)
8	(A) (B) (C) (D)	24	(A) (B) (C) (D)	40	(A) (B) (C) (D)
9	(A) (B) (C) (D)	25	(A) (B) (C) (D)	41	(A) (B) (C) (D)
10	(A) (B) (C) (D)	26	(A) (B) (C) (D)	42	(A) (B) (C) (D)
11	(A) (B) (C) (D)	27	(A) (B) (C) (D)	43	(A) (B) (C) (D)
12	(A) (B) (C) (D)	28	(A) (B) (C) (D)	44	(A) (B) (C) (D)
13	(A) (B) (C) (D)	29	(A) (B) (C) (D)	45	(A) (B) (C) (D)
14	(A) (B) (C) (D)	30	(A) (B) (C) (D)	46	(A) (B) (C) (D)
15	(A) (B) (C) (D)	31	(A) (B) (C) (D)	47	(A) (B) (C) (D)
16	(A) (B) (C) (D)	32	(A) (B) (C) (D)		

Student Name: _____ Grade Applying For: _____

Write in blue or black pen for this essay.

Write your essay topic below

_____
_____
_____

Write your essay below and on the next page

_____
_____
_____
_____
_____
_____
_____
_____
_____
_____
_____
_____
_____
_____
_____
_____
_____
_____
_____
_____
_____

Practice Test 1

Verbal Reasoning

40 questions
20 minutes

The Verbal Reasoning section has two parts. When you finish Part One, be sure to keep working on Part Two. For each answer that you choose, make sure to fill in the corresponding circle on the answer sheet.

Part One – Synonyms

Each question in Part One has a word in capital letters with four answer choices after it. Choose the answer choice with the word that comes closest in meaning to the word in capital letters.

SAMPLE QUESTION:

1. SPEEDY:

   (A) loud
   (B) messy
   ● quick
   (D) small

Part Two – Sentence Completion

Each question in Part Two has a sentence with one or two blanks. Each blank takes the place of a word that is missing. The sentence has four answer choices after it. Choose the answer choice with the word or word pair that best completes the sentence.

SAMPLE QUESTION:

1. Since the weather is getting warmer every day, it is particularly important to -------- more water.

   (A) create
   ● drink
   (C) leave
   (D) waste

STOP

DO NOT BEGIN THE SECTION UNTIL INSTRUCTED TO DO SO

Part One – Synonyms

Directions: Choose the word that is closest in meaning to the word that is in all capital letters.

1. MAGNITUDE:

   (A) attendance
   (B) emotion
   (C) importance
   (D) progression

2. GARRULOUS:

   (A) critical
   (B) endearing
   (C) maudlin
   (D) verbose

3. ERRONEOUS:

   (A) diminished
   (B) inaccurate
   (C) permanent
   (D) unique

4. REMEDY:

   (A) fix
   (B) gain
   (C) handle
   (D) tolerate

5. FOSTER:

   (A) barricade
   (B) encourage
   (C) offer
   (D) spread

6. MASQUERADE:

   (A) disgrace
   (B) nag
   (C) pretend
   (D) stagger

7. INTEGRITY:

   (A) appreciation
   (B) excitement
   (C) hardship
   (D) morals

8. AGGREGATE:

   (A) combine
   (B) hitch
   (C) invent
   (D) shred

9. SEDATE:

   (A) calm
   (B) enclosed
   (C) lanky
   (D) uneasy

10. COLONIZE:

    (A) defy
    (B) outgrow
    (C) position
    (D) settle

CONTINUE TO THE NEXT PAGE

11. TIER:

   (A) amenity
   (B) level
   (C) ravine
   (D) suspension

12. OBDURATE:

   (A) conventional
   (B) feeble
   (C) headstrong
   (D) presumptuous

13. WRETCHED:

   (A) friendly
   (B) living
   (C) pathetic
   (D) rigid

14. TARNISH:

   (A) enact
   (B) preserve
   (C) recruit
   (D) stain

15. SHROUD:

   (A) cover
   (B) ditch
   (C) improve
   (D) snatch

16. LUDICROUS:

   (A) drowsy
   (B) laughable
   (C) painful
   (D) thankful

17. FLAGRANT:

   (A) bold
   (B) uncertain
   (C) entertaining
   (D) subdued

18. TRAVAIL:

   (A) encampment
   (B) misnomer
   (C) pattern
   (D) tribulation

19. IMPECCABLE:

   (A) abundant
   (B) invalid
   (C) perfect
   (D) stunted

CONTINUE TO THE NEXT PAGE

Part Two - Sentence Completion

Directions: Choose the word or word pair that best completes the sentence.

20. Before the -------- of home television sets, people regularly flocked to movie theaters to be entertained.

    (A) advent
    (B) credence
    (C) platitude
    (D) ramification

21. Before author N. Scott Momaday made Native American literature popular by winning the Pulitzer Prize in 1969, many Native American authors struggled to break into the --------.

    (A) commemoration
    (B) imagination
    (C) mainstream
    (D) slump

22. At the Haskell Free Library and Opera House, the actors perform in Canada and the audience sits in the United States because the building -------- the border between the two countries.

    (A) defines
    (B) impairs
    (C) lends
    (D) straddles

23. Although many people believe that the Earth is a fixed distance from the sun, the distance between the two can actually -------- by up to three and a half million miles.

    (A) fade
    (B) include
    (C) reconcile
    (D) vary

CONTINUE TO THE NEXT PAGE

24. In the 1960s, the American bald eagle was rapidly disappearing, but due to laws that protected the species and their habitats the bald eagle is now --------.

    (A) declining
    (B) flourishing
    (C) hesitating
    (D) negligible

25. In 1917, many Russian aristocratic families had to leave the county --------, often only able to take with them the clothes on their back as they fled.

    (A) amazingly
    (B) excitedly
    (C) hastily
    (D) royally

26. Although the use of slang language in published writing used to be quite rare, in more recent times it has become almost --------.

    (A) improvident
    (B) leisurely
    (C) profound
    (D) ubiquitous

27. The number of poison dart frogs living in the wild has declined swiftly as their habitat in the rain forest has been -------- by companies clearing trees.

    (A) acknowledged
    (B) enabled
    (C) ravaged
    (D) sponsored

CONTINUE TO THE NEXT PAGE

28. The goal of the Abbey Theater, established in 1904, was to -------- a revival of Irish dramatic productions and promote Gaelic culture.

   (A) ignite
   (B) label
   (C) profess
   (D) quote

29. During World War I, many members of the Cherokee nation were employed to send and receive messages in their little-known language so that sensitive information would not be revealed if messages were -------- by enemy troops.

   (A) enacted
   (B) intercepted
   (C) occupied
   (D) renewed

30. When awarding contracts, it is important that county officials do not give -------- treatment to bids that are submitted by friends or family members, since this would be considered corruption.

   (A) disorganized
   (B) honorable
   (C) mundane
   (D) preferential

31. With the invention of the personal computer, many people considered typewriters --------, and the typewriter division of the Smith Corona company collapsed.

   (A) accessible
   (B) effective
   (C) superfluous
   (D) tolerable

CONTINUE TO THE NEXT PAGE

32. Many people are -------- of pop musicians and accuse them of producing -------- songs that lack originality.

    (A) disdainful ... derivative
    (B) envious ... judicial
    (C) incredulous ... improvised
    (D) scornful ... novel

33. When creating a sauce with milk and flour, it is -------- that the milk be brought to a boil, otherwise the sauce will not -------- and the result will be a runny mess.

    (A) archaic ... necessitate
    (B) compatible ... intervene
    (C) imperative ... coagulate
    (D) mediocre ... thicken

34. The Buena Vista Social Club provided a(n) -------- place for Cuban musicians to get together and -------- to create jazz infused with the rhythms of traditional Cuban dance music.

    (A) attached ... galvanize
    (B) gathering ... collaborate
    (C) lax ... instill
    (D) temporary ... disagree

35. The professor's -------- appearance hid the fact that she was really a(n) -------- genius.

    (A) emotional ... energetic
    (B) jubilant ... sentimental
    (C) professional ... efficient
    (D) unkempt ... organizational

CONTINUE TO THE NEXT PAGE

36. Although ostriches may look -------- with their skinny legs, they can actually -------- faster than horses.

    (A) attractive ... jog
    (B) camouflaged ... cease
    (C) puny ... sprint
    (D) robust ... race

37. In 1969, the pollution in the Cuyahoga River -------- and the subsequent fire led to greater -------- regulations.

    (A) diminished ... characteristic
    (B) ignited ... environmental
    (C) launched ... machinery
    (D) qualified ... military

38. It is hard to -------- spending additional money on military supplies if there are already -------- provisions in warehouses.

    (A) justify ... surplus
    (B) limit ... excess
    (C) ponder ... scant
    (D) reject ... plentiful

39. Despite the -------- entry to the home, the interior was actually quite --------.

    (A) forgotten ... secure
    (B) lavish ... favorable
    (C) legitimate ... lenient
    (D) resplendent ... dilapidated

40. The man's suddenly -------- behavior caused his acquaintances to -------- their positive opinions of him.

    (A) erratic ... readjust
    (B) genuine ... question
    (C) malicious ... reinforce
    (D) radiant ... eliminate

STOP

IF YOU HAVE TIME LEFT YOU MAY CHECK YOUR ANSWERS IN THIS SECTION ONLY

Quantitative Reasoning

37 questions

35 minutes

Each math question has four answer choices after it. Choose the answer choice that best answers the question.

Make sure that you fill in the correct answer on your answer sheet. You may write in the test booklet.

SAMPLE QUESTION:

1. What is the perimeter of a rectangle with a length of 3 cm and a width of 5 cm?
   $(P = 2l + 2w)$

   (A) 6 cm

   (B) 10 cm

   (C) 8 cm

   ● 16 cm

The correct answer is 16 cm and circle D is filled in.

STOP

DO NOT BEGIN THE SECTION UNTIL INSTRUCTED TO DO SO

Part One – Word Problems

1. If x is an odd integer, then which of the following MUST also be an odd integer?

    (A) $\frac{x+1}{2}$

    (B) $\frac{x+2}{2}$

    (C) $2x - 1$

    (D) $3x + 1$

2. If $\#x\# = 4x - 2$, then what is the value of $\#6\# - \#5\#$?

    (A) 1

    (B) 4

    (C) 18

    (D) 22

3. Triangle ABD is similar to triangle DEF.

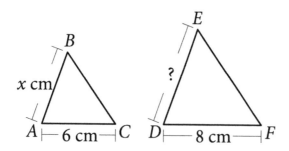

    What is the length of DE?

    (A) $\frac{3}{4}$

    (B) $\frac{4}{3}$

    (C) $\frac{3}{4}x$

    (D) $\frac{4}{3}x$

CONTINUE TO THE NEXT PAGE

4.   If $m + 2 > 2m$, then which could be the value of m?

(A) -100

(B) 2

(C) 5

(D) 10

5.   The mean of a set of four numbers was 18. When a fifth number was added to the set, the mean dropped to 16. What was the number added to the set?

(A) -2

(B) 2

(C) 8

(D) 10

6.   In the figure below a square is inscribed inside a circle.

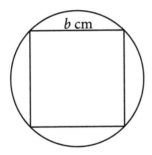

If the square has a side length of b cm, then what is the radius of the circle?

(A) b

(B) $\dfrac{b}{2}$

(C) $\dfrac{b\sqrt{2}}{2}$

(D) $\dfrac{b\sqrt{2}}{4}$

CONTINUE TO THE NEXT PAGE

7.   Mr. Spencer added 6 points to each test score in his class. Which measure of central tendency was affected the least?

(A)   Mean

(B)   Median

(C)   Mode

(D)   Range

8.   Mindy started at the park, walked to her friend Emily's house, and then the two girls walked to the store together. The graph below shows Mindy's distance from the store as a function of time.

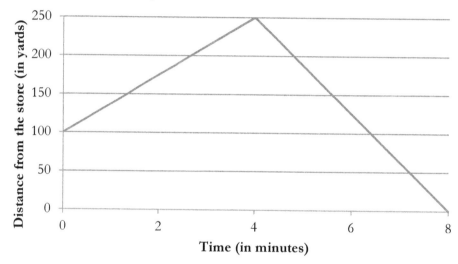

Mindy's distance from the store

If the park, Emily's house, and the store all lie on a straight line, and Mindy walked the shortest distance possible, then how far is the park from Emily's house?

(A)   150 yards

(B)   200 yards

(C)   250 yards

(D)   300 yards

CONTINUE TO THE NEXT PAGE

9.   What is the value of $4 \div 2 + 8 \times (7 - 3) \div 4$?

   (A) 8
   (B) 10
   (C) 12
   (D) 24

10.   The figure below shows two squares.

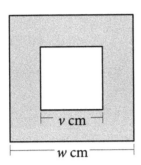

   What is the area of the shaded region?

   (A) $w - v$ cm^2
   (B) $v - w$ cm^2
   (C) $w^2 - v^2$ cm^2
   (D) $v^2 - w^2$ cm^2

11.   If $\sqrt{b + c} = 6$, then which of the following must be true?

   (A) $\sqrt{b} + \sqrt{c} = 6$
   (B) $b + c = 6$
   (C) $b^2 + c^2 = 36$
   (D) $b + c = 36$

CONTINUE TO THE NEXT PAGE

12. The Stokes family spent $4,000 on a trip. The circle graph below shows how their money was spent.

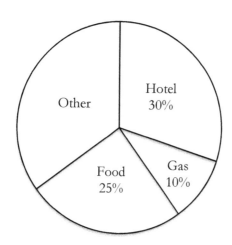

How much money did the Stokes family spend on "other" expenses?

(A) $1,000

(B) $1,400

(C) $1,800

(D) $2,000

13. The box-and-whisker plot below represents the number of flights delayed each day for one month at a single airport.

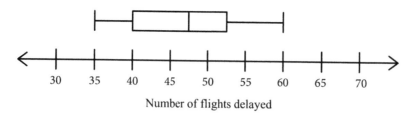

Number of flights delayed

Which measure could not be equal to one of the data points?

(A) mean

(B) median

(C) mode

(D) range

CONTINUE TO THE NEXT PAGE

14. The area of a triangle can be found using the formula $area = \frac{1}{2}bh$, where b is the length of the base and h is the height of the triangle. If the area of a triangle is 28 cm^2 and the base length is 8 cm, then which equation could be used to find the height?

(A) $h = \frac{8 \times 2}{28}$

(B) $h = \frac{28}{8 \times 2}$

(C) $h = \frac{28}{8} \times \frac{1}{2}$

(D) $h = \frac{28 \times 2}{8}$

15. The inequality $|h - 40| < 10$ gives the range of allowable heights for riders on a carousel, in inches. A child of which height would NOT be allowed to ride on the carousel?

(A) 31 inches

(B) 36 inches

(C) 40 inches

(D) 51 inches

16. If the width of a rectangle is increased by 20 percent and the length is decreased by 30 percent, by what percent is the area of the rectangle decreased?

(A) 10%

(B) 16%

(C) 20%

(D) 24%

CONTINUE TO THE NEXT PAGE

17. Line g is perpendicular to line h. If the equation of line g is $y = \frac{3}{4}x + 6$, which could be the equation of line h?

   (A) $y = \frac{3}{4}x + 8$

   (B) $y = -\frac{3}{4}x + 6$

   (C) $y = \frac{4}{3}x - 3$

   (D) $y = -\frac{4}{3}x - 11$

18. Which is equal to the value of the expression $\dfrac{25(5^3 + 25)}{125(5 + 5^2)}$?

   (A) 0

   (B) $\dfrac{1}{5}$

   (C) 1

   (D) 5

19. If $\frac{1}{3}n + \frac{2}{6} = m$, then which is equal to the value of n?

   (A) $3m - 1$
   (B) $3m - 2$
   (C) $6m - 1$
   (D) $6m + 2$

CONTINUE TO THE NEXT PAGE

Part Two – Quantitative Comparisons

Directions: Use the information in the question to compare the quantities in Columns A and B. After comparing the two quantities, choose the correct answer choice:

(A) Quantity in Column A is greater.
(B) Quantity in Column B is greater.
(C) The quantities in Column A and Column B are equal.
(D) Cannot be determined from information given.

	Column A	Column B
20.	1,000 m	0.001 km

Mr. Shaw added 4 points to each of the test scores in his class.

	Column A	Column B
21.	The change to the mean test score	The change to the median test score

Ann has $1.60 in dimes and nickels. She has twice as many nickels as dimes. (Note: 1 dime = $0.10 and 1 nickel = $0.05)

	Column A	Column B
22.	The total value of the dimes	The total value of the nickels

Margaret is thinking of an integer that is greater than 11 but less than 15. The number is also greater than 9 but less than 14.

	Column A	Column B
23.	The number of possible values of the integer that Margaret is thinking of	3

CONTINUE TO THE NEXT PAGE

The box-and-whisker plot below represents the average high temperature each day in one month in City X.

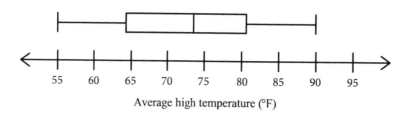

Average high temperature (°F)

Column A	**Column B**
24. The mean high temperature	The median high temperature

Column A	**Column B**
25. $6(v-1)$	$6v-1$

The graph below shows the population of five different towns located in the same valley.

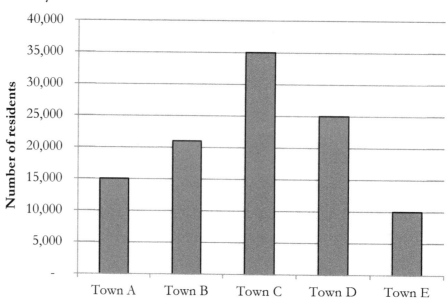

Column A	**Column B**
26. The median population	35,000

CONTINUE TO THE NEXT PAGE

	Column A	Column B
27.	6	$16 + 8 \div (1 + 3)$

A random number generator prints numbers 1 through 9. It is going to print two numbers.

	Column A	Column B
28.	The probability that it will print 8 and then 8	The probability that it will print 8 and then 4

The area of a field is 100 square yards.

	Column A	Column B
29.	The length of a fence that goes around the perimeter of the field	40 yards

w is any real number.

	Column A	Column B
30.	w	$\dfrac{1}{w}$

A candy dish contains 8 red candies, 12 green candies, and 10 yellow candies. Two candies are randomly selected from the dish.

	Column A	Column B
31.	The probability that at least one of the candies is red	The probability that both candies are red

	Column A	Column B
32.	$(x + 2)(x - 3)$	$x^2 + x - 6$

CONTINUE TO THE NEXT PAGE

	Column A	Column B
33.	$\left(\dfrac{1}{3}\right)^{-20}$	$\left(\dfrac{1}{3}\right)^{-\frac{1}{20}}$

The area of a circle with radius r is $A = \pi r^2$.

	Column A	Column B
34.	The area of a circle with a radius $x + 1$ cm long	$(x^2 + 1)\pi$

A coin is going to be flipped 10 times.

	Column A	Column B
35.	If the coin lands heads up on the first 9 coin tosses, the probability that the coin will land heads up on the 10th toss	If the coin lands heads up on at least 4 of the first 9 tosses, the probability that the coin will land heads up on the 10th toss

A jar contains 10 black stones and 10 white stones. Two stones are to be randomly selected.

	Column A	Column B
36.	The probability that both stones will be white if the first stone is replaced before the second stone is drawn	The probability that both stones will be white if the first stone is NOT replaced before the second stone is drawn

	Column A	Column B
37.	$(0.8)^{18}$	$(0.8)^{19}$

STOP

IF YOU HAVE TIME LEFT YOU MAY CHECK YOUR ANSWERS IN THIS SECTION ONLY

Reading Comprehension

36 questions
35 minutes

The Reading Comprehension section has six short passages. Each passage has six questions after it. For each question, choose the answer choice that comes closest to what is stated or implied in the passage. You may write in the test booklet.

STOP
DO NOT BEGIN THE SECTION UNTIL INSTRUCTED TO DO SO

Questions #1-6

1   In July of 1863, Union troops took to a battlefield in Gettysburg, Pennsylvania, in
2 order to bury those who had perished in battle. As they worked, they made a startling
3 discovery. Among the soldiers that they were interring, there was a woman dressed in
4 a Confederate uniform. At this time, women were not allowed to fight in either the
5 Union or Confederate armies.
6   Over time, more and more women who disguised their gender to fight in the
7 American Civil War have been uncovered. Historians now believe that there could have
8 been over 400 women who passed as male soldiers in both the Union and Confederate
9 armies.
10   The social attitudes of the time helped explain how women were able to blend into
11 the ranks of an all-male army. During the 1860s in the United States, modesty was
12 considered a virtue. Men kept their bodies covered, bathed separately, and avoided
13 public bathrooms. Often women were only discovered when they were injured and
14 receiving medical care.
15   The motivations for these female soldiers were varied. Some women were driven
16 to the battlefield by the despair they felt in not being help the war cause. Sarah Emma
17 Edmonds disguised herself as Franklin Flint Thompson and fought because she "could
18 only thank God that I was free and could go forward and work, and I was not obliged to
19 stay home and weep."
20   Some other women felt that their rightful place was among male colleagues. One
21 of the most famous of the women who fought as male soldiers was Jennie Hodgers. She
22 was only eighteen when she joined the Union army and served a three-year enlistment.
23 After the war, she returned to her home state of Illinois and continued to live as a man,
24 taking jobs such as farmhand, janitor, and streetlamp lighter. In November of 1910,
25 when she was sixty-eight years old, she was struck by a car, and her gender was revealed
26 at the hospital. Many of her former fellow soldiers protested for her right to maintain a
27 male identity. Due to their efforts, when she died in 1915, she was buried in full uniform
28 and given a tombstone that reflected her male identity.
29   The contribution of these women was much greater than their numbers. Feminist
30 leaders such as Susan B. Anthony and Elizabeth Cady Stanton used the bravery of these
31 women to show that women deserved the same right to participate in American
32 government. Clara Barton, famous as a nurse during the Civil War, noted the
33 contribution of women both on and off the field when she claimed that the four-year
34 war period advanced the social position of women at least fifty years.

CONTINUE TO THE NEXT PAGE

1. The main purpose of this passage is to

    (A) provide information about the causes of the Civil War.
    (B) describe the contribution of a particular group during the Civil War.
    (C) refute a commonly held belief.
    (D) describe differences between the women in the two armies.

2. In line 8, the word "passed" is used to mean

    (A) disguised.
    (B) went by.
    (C) impressed.
    (D) mourned.

3. According to the passage, some women were inspired to hide their identities and join the army because

    (A) there were few other opportunities for women.
    (B) their fathers and husbands encouraged them.
    (C) they possessed superior rifle skills.
    (D) the alternative was to spend their life mourning at home.

4. In the fourth paragraph (lines 15-19), the author states that Jennie Hodgers was buried in full uniform because

    (A) she served two enlistments in the Union army.
    (B) she had lived as a man for many years.
    (C) her comrades argued for her right to be buried in uniform.
    (D) there was a change in the laws.

5. The author suggests that Clara Barton believed that female participation in the Civil War

    (A) led to unnecessary casualties.
    (B) affected the social standing of women.
    (C) undermined the efforts of feminists.
    (D) remains unrecognized.

6. The author includes the last paragraph (lines 29-34) in order to

    (A) provide information about other women who took part in the Civil War.
    (B) compare and contrast two different groups.
    (C) discuss the role of women in the army.
    (D) provide context for understanding the importance of women soldiers in the Civil War.

CONTINUE TO THE NEXT PAGE

Questions #7-12

In the passage below, former American president Theodore Roosevelt shares a recollection from his own childhood.

1   Now and then we children were taken round to our grandfather's house; a big
2   house for the New York of those days, on the corner of Fourteenth Street and Broadway,
3   fronting Union Square. Inside there was a large hall running up to the roof; there was a
4   tessellated black-and-white marble floor, and a circular staircase round the sides of the
5   hall, from the top floor down. We children much admired both the tessellated floor and
6   the circular staircase. I think we were right about the latter, but I am not so sure as to
7   the tessellated floor.
8   The summers we spent in the country, now at one place, now at another. We
9   children, of course, loved the country beyond anything. We disliked the city. We were
10   always wildly eager to get to the country when spring came, and very sad when in the
11   late fall the family moved back to town. In the country we of course had all kinds of
12   pets – cats, dogs, rabbits, a coon, and a sorrel Shetland pony named General Grant.
13   When my younger sister first heard of the real General Grant, by the way, she was much
14   struck by the coincidence that some one should have given him the same name as the
15   pony. (Thirty years later my own children had their pony Grant.) In the country we
16   children ran barefoot much of the time, and the seasons went by in a round of
17   uninterrupted and enthralling pleasures – supervising the haying and harvesting,
18   picking apples, hunting frogs successfully and woodchucks unsuccessfully, gathering
19   hickory-nuts and chestnuts for sale to patient parents, building wigwams in the woods,
20   and sometimes playing Indians in too realistic manner by staining ourselves (and
21   incidentally our clothes) in liberal fashion with poke-cherry juice. Thanksgiving was an
22   appreciated festival, but it in no way came up to Christmas. Christmas was an occasion
23   of literally delirious joy. In the evening we hung up our stockings – or rather the biggest
24   stockings we could borrow from the grown-ups – and before dawn we trooped in to
25   open them while sitting on father's and mother's bed; and the bigger presents were
26   arranged, those for each child on its own table, in the drawing-room, the doors to which
27   were thrown open after breakfast. I never knew any one else have what seemed to me
28   such attractive Christmases, and in the next generation I tried to reproduce them exactly
29   for my own children.

---

7.   The main purpose of this passage is to

(A)   describe one person's experience.
(B)   explain holiday customs in America.
(C)   provide information on pet care.
(D)   encourage a course of action.

CONTINUE TO THE NEXT PAGE

8. In line 17, the word "enthralling" most nearly means

    (A) banal.
    (B) fascinating.
    (C) limitless.
    (D) stunted.

9. The author describes his grandfather's house as

    (A) formal.
    (B) in the country.
    (C) maintained by servants.
    (D) where the author celebrated Christmas.

10. In the final sentence (lines 27-29), the author suggests that his children

    (A) are annoyed by his attempts to recreate his childhood.
    (B) prefer to go to the country as well.
    (C) live in the city.
    (D) had Christmas experiences that were similar to those of the author.

11. The author implies that his sister believed that

    (A) all ponies are named General Grant.
    (B) General Grant was a common name for pets.
    (C) the actual General Grant was named after their pony.
    (D) every child has a pony.

12. In line 19, the author describes his parents as "patient" because they

    (A) put up with noisy children.
    (B) were bored at their country house.
    (C) played games with their children endlessly.
    (D) bought chestnuts and hickory-nuts that they didn't actually want.

CONTINUE TO THE NEXT PAGE

Questions #13-18

The following passage is adapted from "Tea Drinking in 18ᵗʰ-Century America: Its Etiquette and Equipage" by Rodris Roth.

1   English customs were generally imitated in this country, particularly in the urban
2   centers. Of Boston, where he visited in 1740, Joseph Bennett observed that "the ladies
3   here visit, drink tea and indulge every little piece of gentility to the height of the mode
4   and neglect the affairs of their families with as good grace as the finest ladies in London."
5   English modes and manners remained a part of the social behavior after the colonies
6   became an independent nation. Visitors to the newly formed United States were apt to
7   remark about such habits as tea drinking, as did Brissot de Warville in 1788, that "in
8   this, as in their whole manner of living, the Americans in general resemble the English."
9   Therefore, it is not surprising to find that during the 18th century the serving of tea
10   privately in the morning and socially in the afternoon or early evening was an
11   established custom in many households.
12   The naturalist Peter Kalm, during his visit to North America in the mid-18th
13   century, noted that tea was a breakfast beverage in both Pennsylvania and New York.
14   From the predominantly Dutch town of Albany in 1749 he wrote that "their breakfast
15   is tea, commonly without milk." At another time, Kalm stated:

16   *With the tea was eaten bread and butter or buttered bread toasted over*
17   *the coals so that the butter penetrated the whole slice of bread. In the*
18   *afternoon about three o'clock tea was drunk again in the same fashion,*
19   *except that bread and butter was not served with it.*

20   This tea-drinking schedule was followed throughout the colonies. In Boston the
21   people "take a great deal of tea in the morning," have dinner at two o'clock, and "about
22   five o'clock they take more tea, some wine, madeira [and] punch," reported the Baron
23   Cromot du Bourg during his visit in 1781. The Marquis de Chastellux confirms his
24   countryman's statement about teatime, mentioning that the Americans take "tea and
25   punch in the afternoon."
26   During the first half of the 18th century the limited amount of tea available at
27   prohibitively high prices restricted its use to a proportionately small segment of the total
28   population of the colonies. About mid-century, however, tea was beginning to be drunk
29   by more and more people, as supplies increased and costs decreased, due in part to the
30   propaganda and merchandising efforts of the East India Company. According to Peter
31   Kalm, tea, chocolate, and coffee had been "wholly unknown" to the Swedish population
32   of Pennsylvania and the surrounding area before the English arrived, but in 1748 these
33   beverages "at present constitute even the country people's daily breakfast."

CONTINUE TO THE NEXT PAGE

13. The primary purpose of this passage is to

   (A) explain how tea became an important drink in the American colonies.
   (B) describe the importance of the East India Company to the development of American culture.
   (C) criticize the habits of early colonists.
   (D) provide an overview of life in colonial America.

14. The author states that tea became common to drink only when

   (A) it was introduced to Pennsylvania.
   (B) wine became limited.
   (C) the English introduced it to the colonies.
   (D) the cost of tea was reduced.

15. The author most likely quotes Baron Cromot du Bourg, the Marquis de Chastellux, and Peter Kalm in order to

   (A) incorporate the opinions of tea experts.
   (B) provide the viewpoints of outside observers.
   (C) emphasize the influence of other countries on the habits of Americans.
   (D) provide a counterpoint to the main argument.

16. It can be inferred from the passage that in Sweden

   (A) immigration was common.
   (B) tea was not a common breakfast drink.
   (C) tea was drunk without milk.
   (D) chocolate was unheard of.

17. Joseph Bennett's attitude toward women in Boston can best be described as

   (A) pure admiration.
   (B) limited optimism.
   (C) condescending.
   (D) openly hostile.

18. The passage suggests that tea in the afternoon was

   (A) a social experience in early America.
   (B) frequently served with buttered toast.
   (C) often mixed with wine to create a punch.
   (D) curtailed by the East India Company.

CONTINUE TO THE NEXT PAGE

Questions #19-24

1   In June of 2013, President Barack Obama stood in the sweltering heat of
2 Washington, D.C. and declared that something must be done to "put an end to the
3 limitless dumping of carbon pollution from our power plants." This speech was cheered
4 by environmentalists, but derided by the operators of coal-fired power plants. Plants
5 that burn coal produce twice the carbon dioxide of those that burn natural gas. Carbon
6 dioxide in the atmosphere has been pinpointed as a cause of global warming. Burning
7 coal also sprays particulate matter into the atmosphere, leading to thick smog and a host
8 of human health issues.
9   It isn't as simple as blaming the coal industry, however. Coal plants supply roughly
10 40% of the world's energy, and energy use shows no signs of shrinking. Coal is the
11 dirtiest energy source that we have available, but it is also the cheapest. In addition, it
12 is readily available in many of the places where demand for electricity is high.
13   One technology that has promise for improving the situation is capturing some of
14 the carbon dioxide that is produced in the coal burning process. In carbon capturing,
15 the smoke produced is forced through a system that separates out the carbon dioxide
16 and then compresses the gas. The question then becomes what to do with this
17 compressed carbon dioxide. In many places, this byproduct of carbon dioxide is then
18 injected deep in the ground into porous rock formations.
19   American Electric Power's coal-fired Mountaineer Plant in New Haven, West
20 Virginia, pioneered a carbon capturing system. The plant set up an experimental carbon
21 capture system that processed about 1.5% of the gas produced and was highly effective
22 in removing carbon matter. The company was set to scale up the operation, and
23 scientists and energy executives came from all over the world to study their system. The
24 issue, however, was that this technology does not come free. It cost nothing to continue
25 polluting the environment, but American Electric Power would have had to charge
26 more for the energy produced with the carbon scrubbing system in place. Ultimately,
27 regulators did not allow the company to raise rates to cover the cost of this technology,
28 and in 2011 the system was dismantled.
29   One solution that has been proposed is to charge a "carbon-tax" for the pollution
30 released into the atmosphere. Proponents of this system argue that by increasing the
31 cost of "doing nothing", it is easier to justify the cost of installing technology that
32 removes carbon dioxide from plant emissions. Opponents of this proposal point out
33 that this would raise energy costs for everyone, which would disproportionately affect
34 lower income families who tend to spend a higher percentage of their income on energy.

CONTINUE TO THE NEXT PAGE

19. The main purpose of this passage is to

   (A) demonstrate ways that carbon capturing systems work.
   (B) present various issues surrounding coal-fired power plants.
   (C) illustrate the reluctance of power companies to switch from burning coal to using an alternate source of fuel.
   (D) provide consumers with the information necessary to make a choice about their electricity supplier.

20. In line 4, the word "derided" most nearly means

   (A) described.
   (B) ignored.
   (C) scoffed at.
   (D) supported.

21. Which conclusion does the author most likely want the reader to make from the description of the Mountaineer Plant (lines 19-28)?

   (A) A carbon capture system is not a realistic solution because it can only process a small portion of the gas produced by burning coal.
   (B) Lower income families have trouble affording energy from the Mountaineer Plant.
   (C) The carbon scrubbing system produced a byproduct that was just as bad as the carbon dioxide released into the atmosphere.
   (D) The pricing of energy stopped a company from using a technology that leads to less carbon dioxide in the atmosphere.

22. What is the most likely reason that many countries continue to use coal-fired plants instead of plants that burn natural gas?

   (A) Electricity can be produced less expensively at coal-fired plants.
   (B) Natural gas is hard to obtain.
   (C) Pollution is of no concern to power companies.
   (D) Regulators make it hard to convert a power plant from coal to natural gas.

23. Which is the best description of the organization of this passage?

   (A) A thesis is presented and then refuted.
   (B) Various issues in a complex problem are presented and a solution is suggested.
   (C) A problem is introduced and then illustrations are presented.
   (D) Two conflicting viewpoints are presented and evaluated.

CONTINUE TO THE NEXT PAGE

24. Why does the author propose a tax on carbon emissions?

(A) If companies paid for the carbon dioxide released, then the relative cost of carbon scrubbing would be less.

(B) It isn't fair for some companies to pollute more than other companies.

(C) Lower income families would bear less of the cost of energy production.

(D) It would make electricity produced in plants with carbon scrubbers cost less than electricity produced in plants without them.

Questions #25-30

1   Sweden is a land of contrasts, particularly when it comes to climate. Due to how
2   far north Sweden lies, it experiences some of the longest summer days as well as some
3   of the shortest winter days. Many holidays important to Swedish people celebrate the
4   arrival or disappearance of the sun.
5   One of these holidays is Lucia Night, which is celebrated on December 13. Before
6   Sweden adopted the modern calendar, December 13 was the night of the winter solstice,
7   which falls on the longest night of the year. In Swedish folklore, it was believed that the
8   long night would bring out supernatural beings and other dark forces. It was also a
9   night when animals could speak. The morning after Lucia Night, both animals and
10 people would be exhausted and need to eat a hearty breakfast.
11   Over time, the tradition evolved so that young women would be named Lucia, or
12 the bearer of light. Lucia was a mythical figure who bore light in the long, dark Swedish
13 winter nights. The first reference of a young woman dressing all in white to represent
14 Lucia comes from 1764. By the 1880s, young women dressed as Lucia began serving the
15 buns and coffee as part of the breakfast celebration after Lucia Night. In the 1900s, the
16 tradition of a young woman dressed as Lucia gained popularity and competitions began
17 for who would be named Lucia. It is now common for each town to name one girl as
18 Lucia. A couple of weeks before Lucia Night, the local newspaper prints a ballot for
19 potential Lucia candidates, and the readers of the newspaper elect the winner. The lucky
20 girl gets to ride around town in a horse-drawn vehicle to share songs and spread light.
21 There is also a national Lucia who is named on one of the television networks.

25. The primary purpose of this passage is to

(A) describe a cultural event.

(B) provide context for an argument.

(C) demonstrate the importance of local traditions.

(D) prove that better record keeping is needed for local folktales.

CONTINUE TO THE NEXT PAGE

26. According to the passage, which is true about Lucia Night?

    (A) It began as a celebration of light.
    (B) Other countries have adopted the Lucia Night celebration.
    (C) It ends with a sleigh ride through town.
    (D) It was originally believed that animals could talk on Lucia Night.

27. The author implies that Sweden

    (A) has named Lucia Night as an official state holiday.
    (B) no longer celebrates Lucia Night on the shortest day of the year.
    (C) strictly limits the number of Lucias that can be elected.
    (D) rarely initiates new traditions.

28. According to the passage, countries that are far north

    (A) all have traditions that celebrate light.
    (B) do not use the modern calendar.
    (C) have longer summer days than countries that are closer to the equator.
    (D) consist mainly of rural farms.

29. In line 8, the word "supernatural" most nearly means

    (A) not produced by man.
    (B) unexplainable by natural laws.
    (C) not classified as an animal.
    (D) goblins.

30. The primary purpose of the second paragraph (lines 5-10) is to

    (A) introduce a new topic.
    (B) explain how Lucia Night became a celebration of light.
    (C) create a sense of suspense to engage the reader.
    (D) provide historical context for a modern celebration.

CONTINUE TO THE NEXT PAGE

Questions #31-36

1   On October 17, 1956, the "game of the century" was played at the Rosenwald
2   Memorial Tournament in New York City. It was not a baseball or football game, but
3   rather it was a chess match for the history books. Donald Byrne was favored to win. He
4   was a recognized chess master who had won the U.S. Open Championship in 1953. His
5   opponent was a thirteen-year-old boy: Bobby Fischer.
6   Few people expected Bobby Fischer to win, but he had the confidence of a young
7   person who had yet to really experience failure. During the game, Bobby Fischer
8   showed a disregard for the "right" way to play chess. Instead, he incorporated his own
9   innovations and was able to triumph over an opponent who was roughly twice his age.
10   From there, he went on to become a phenomenal player who couldn't seem to lose.
11   The same spirit that allowed him to disregard the conventional rules of chess also
12   led him down the path of a turbulent life. He was known for making horrific comments
13   about groups of people, including women and Jews. He continued to travel the world
14   to play chess but frequently ran afoul of his host countries. In 1992, he scheduled a
15   match against Boris Spassky in Yugoslavia. The U.S. Department of Treasury warned
16   Fischer that he would be in violation of U.S. law if he were to play in the match due to
17   sanctions that were in place at the time forbidding economic activities in Yugoslavia.
18   He played anyway, and as a result, a warrant was issued for his arrest. He became a
19   fugitive and was arrested in Japan 12 years after he played the game. His saving grace
20   was that Iceland granted him asylum and allowed him to become an Icelandic citizen.
21   He remained in Iceland until his death in 2008.
22   Some people view Bobby Fischer as the greatest chess player who ever lived.
23   Others view him as a cautionary tale of what happens to children who experience
24   success at an age when they are not yet capable of handling it. The truth is that both
25   characterizations are accurate.

---

31.   Which best states the main idea of this passage?

(A)   Bobby Fischer won many chess tournaments.
(B)   Bobby Fischer was a brilliant but complicated man.
(C)   Competitive chess provides a forum where children can succeed.
(D)   It is tragic that Bobby Fischer got caught up in a conflict between two countries.

CONTINUE TO THE NEXT PAGE

32. The phrase "led him down the path" (line 12) most nearly means

 (A) showed him how to take a journey.
 (B) provided an example of how to live.
 (C) took the first step toward a goal.
 (D) pointed his life in a certain direction.

33. In line 12, the word "turbulent" most nearly means

 (A) chaotic.
 (B) fulfilled.
 (C) successful.
 (D) unsatisfied.

34. The passage implies that Bobby Fischer considered the U.S. government's authority to be

 (A) absolute.
 (B) at times too strict.
 (C) not worthy of respect.
 (D) a symbol of greatness.

35. A cautionary tale (line 23) can best be described as a story

 (A) without a true ending.
 (B) passed down from one generation to the next.
 (C) designed to teach a moral lesson.
 (D) without a known author.

36. The author most likely includes the first paragraph (lines 1-5) in order to

 (A) heighten the reader's interest in Bobby Fischer.
 (B) describe Bobby Fischer's childhood.
 (C) illustrate the importance of the "game of the century".
 (D) establish the time period that Bobby Fischer lived in.

STOP

IF YOU HAVE TIME LEFT YOU MAY CHECK YOUR ANSWERS IN THIS SECTION ONLY

Mathematics Achievement

47 questions
40 minutes

Each math question has four answer choices after it. Choose the answer choice that best answers the question.

Make sure that you fill in the correct answer on your answer sheet. You may write in the test booklet.

SAMPLE QUESTION:

1. Which number can be divided by 4 with nothing left over?

    (A) 6
    ● 12
    (C) 15
    (D) 22

Since 12 can be divided by 4 with no remainder, circle B is filled in.

STOP

DO NOT BEGIN THE SECTION UNTIL INSTRUCTED TO DO SO

1. The graph below shows the ages of students registered for a summer camp. The numbers on the horizontal axis represent the ages of the campers and the numbers on the vertical axis represent the number of campers of that age.

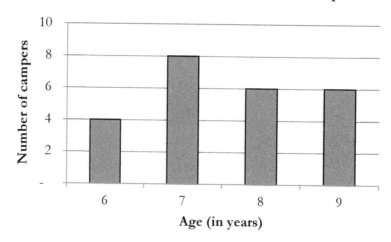

What is the median age of the campers?

(A) 7 years

(B) 7.5 years

(C) 8 years

(D) 8.5 years

2. The mean height of five children is 56 inches. The heights of three of the children are 58 inches, 55 inches, and 53 inches. What must be the mean height for the remaining two children?

(A) 57 inches

(B) 58 inches

(C) 60 inches

(D) 114 inches

3. A flagpole that is 25 meters high casts a shadow that is 32 meters long. A man is standing next to the flagpole and casts a shadow that is 2.4 meters long. How many meters tall is the man?

(A) 1.5

(B) 1.75

(C) 1.875

(D) 2.0

CONTINUE TO THE NEXT PAGE

4. What value(s) of b make $\frac{(b-4)(b-5)}{b^2-16}$ equal to zero?

(A) $b = 5$ only

(B) $b = 5$ or $b = 4$

(C) $b = -4$ or $b = 4$

(D) $b = -4, b = 4,$ or $b = 5$

5. Triangle LMN is shown below. The length of $\overline{LN}$ is 6 and the measure of angle LMN is 65°.

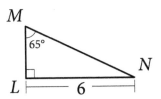

The value of which expression is equal to the length of $\overline{LM}$?

(A) $\dfrac{\tan 65°}{6}$

(B) $\dfrac{6}{\tan 65°}$

(C) $\dfrac{\sin 65°}{6}$

(D) $\dfrac{6}{\sin 65°}$

6. If B is an odd number, then which of the following products MUST also be an odd number?

(A) $B(B + 2)$

(B) $(B + 1)(B - 1)$

(C) $(B + 2)(B - 1)$

(D) $(B + 3)(B - 1)$

CONTINUE TO THE NEXT PAGE

7. Neil asked the students in his class how many days this week they bought lunch in the cafeteria. The results are shown in the table below.

MEALS BOUGHT IN CAFETERIA

Number of meals bought in cafeteria	Number of students who bought that number of meals this week
0	3
1	6
2	5
3	7
4	4

What is the mode of this data?

(A) 1

(B) 2

(C) 3

(D) 7

8. A quadrilateral is shown below.

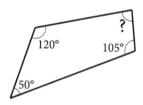

What is the measure of the fourth angle?

(A) 70°

(B) 80°

(C) 85°

(D) 95°

CONTINUE TO THE NEXT PAGE

9.   If $mn + 4 = -lm$, then what is m equal to?

(A) $\dfrac{n+l}{4}$

(B) $\dfrac{n+l}{-4}$

(C) $\dfrac{-4}{n+l}$

(D) $\dfrac{4}{n+l}$

10. The circle below is inscribed in a square. It has a radius of 4 cm.

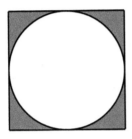

What is the area of the shaded region?

(A) $(16 - 4\pi)$ cm^2

(B) $(16 - 8\pi)$ cm^2

(C) $(64 - 8\pi)$ cm^2

(D) $(64 - 16\pi)$ cm^2

CONTINUE TO THE NEXT PAGE

11. The graph below shows the number of buttons created by a machine over time. The horizontal axis shows the number of hours the machine has been operating and the vertical axis shows the total number of buttons produced.

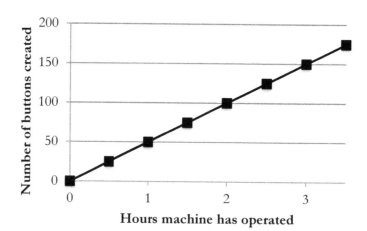

If the machine starts operating at 9:00 AM, and continues at the same rate without stopping, at what time will it have produced 375 buttons?

(A) 3:45 PM

(B) 4:00 PM

(C) 4:15 PM

(D) 4:30 PM

12. What is the product of $6i$ and $3i$?

(A) $9i$

(B) $18i$

(C) 18

(D) -18

CONTINUE TO THE NEXT PAGE

13. Shane leaves him home at 1 PM, drives due west for 2 hours, and then drives due north for 2 hours. If he drives at a constant speed, which graph could represent his distance from home?

(A)

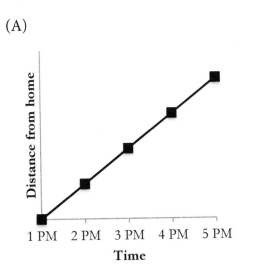

(B)

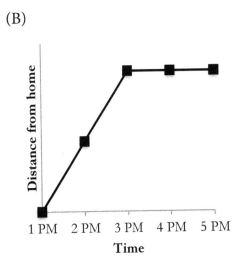

(C)

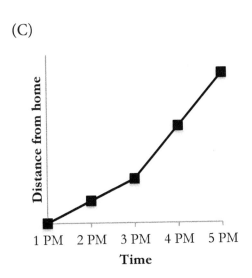

(D)

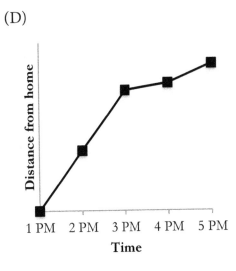

CONTINUE TO THE NEXT PAGE

14. The figure below was created by adding a semi-circle to an equilateral triangle with a side length of 4 cm.

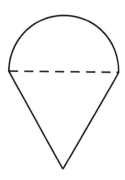

What is the perimeter of this figure?

(A) $4 + 2\pi$ cm

(B) $4 + 4\pi$ cm

(C) $8 + 2\pi$ cm

(D) $8 + 4\pi$ cm

15. What is the greatest common factor of $8x^2y^4$ and $12x^5y^3$?

(A) $2x^2y^3$

(B) $4x^2y^3$

(C) $24x^2y^3$

(D) $24x^5y^4$

CONTINUE TO THE NEXT PAGE

16.   The figure below has all right angles.

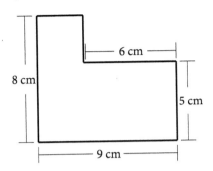

What is the area of the figure?

(A)   36 cm²

(B)   54 cm²

(C)   64 cm²

(D)   72 cm²

17.   If $\dfrac{25(x+50)}{75} = 2x$, then what is the value of x?

(A) $\dfrac{2}{5}$

(B) $\dfrac{5}{2}$

(C)   5

(D)   10

CONTINUE TO THE NEXT PAGE

18.   The circle graph below shows the Barrett family budget.

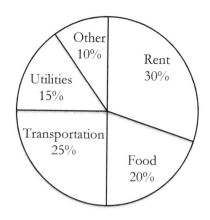

If the Barretts expect to pay $210 each month for utilities, how much do they expect to pay for transportation each month?

(A) $270

(B) $350

(C) $400

(D) $420

19.   The table below shows a pattern.

X	Y
1	4
2	6
3	8
...	...
...	...
...	...
m	g

If the pattern shown above continues, then $g =$

(A) $2m + 2$

(B) $2(m + 2)$

(C) $4m$

(D) $5m - 1$

CONTINUE TO THE NEXT PAGE

20. The stem and leaf plot below shows the scores on a science test.

6	8	9	9	9						
7	1	1	3	4	6	6	6	7	9	
8	0	0	0	0	1	2	3	5	5	6	8
9	2	2	2	5	6	7	8	8	9	

What is the mode of this data?

(A) 0
(B) 9
(C) 80
(D) 81

21. What is the least common multiple of $12g$, $9gh^2$, and $6h^3$, if g and h are prime numbers?

(A) $3g$
(B) $3gh^2$
(C) $36gh^3$
(D) $36g^2h^5$

22. The box-and-whisker plot below represents the number of days that it rained in January at a certain location for each of the last 30 years.

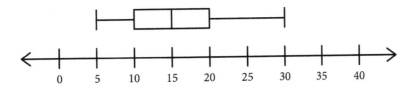

What is the median of this data?

(A) 5
(B) 10
(C) 15
(D) 25

CONTINUE TO THE NEXT PAGE

23. Each grid square shown below is 4 cm².

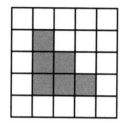

What is the area of the shaded region?

(A) 4 cm²

(B) 6 cm²

(C) 12 cm²

(D) 24 cm²

24. When $-2m$ is subtracted from $-4m$, the result is

(A) $-6m$

(B) $-2m$

(C) $2m$

(D) $6m$

25. The volume of a cylinder can be found using the formula $V = \pi r^2 h$, where r is the radius of the cylinder and h is the height of the cylinder. A cylindrical pipe has a diameter of 6 inches and a length of 24 inches. If the pipe is $\frac{2}{3}$ full of water, then what is the volume of the water in the pipe, in inches³?

(A) 72π

(B) 84π

(C) 144π

(D) 576π

CONTINUE TO THE NEXT PAGE

26. Which value is NOT equal to $\frac{1}{3} + \frac{1}{3}$?

    (A) $\frac{2}{3}$

    (B) $\frac{3}{4.5}$

    (C) $0.666666\overline{6}$

    (D) 0.6666667

27. The price of meat increased from \$3.00 to \$4.50. What was the percent increase in the price of meat?

    (A) 33%
    (B) 40%
    (C) 50%
    (D) 60%

28. For what values of x does $\frac{x}{3} \times \frac{3}{x} = 1$?

    (A) 1
    (B) 3
    (C) all real numbers
    (D) all real numbers except 0

CONTINUE TO THE NEXT PAGE

29. The graph of a line is shown below.

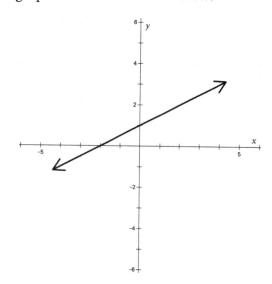

What is the equation of this line?

(A) $y = -2x + 1$

(B) $y = -\frac{1}{2}x + 1$

(C) $y = \frac{1}{2}x - 2$

(D) $y = \frac{1}{2}x + 1$

30. What are the possible values of x if $|x| > 6$?

(A) $x > -6$ only

(B) $x > 6$ only

(C) $-6 < x < 6$

(D) $x > 6$ or $x < -6$

CONTINUE TO THE NEXT PAGE

31. The graph below shows the solution set of an inequality.

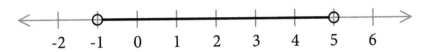

Which inequality is represented by this graph?

(A) $|x + 2| < 3$
(B) $|x - 2| < 3$
(C) $|x + 3| < 2$
(D) $|x - 3| < 2$

32. Which is equivalent to the value of the expression $9^{10}(3^5)$?

(A) 3^{15}
(B) 3^{20}
(C) 3^{25}
(D) 3^{100}

33. What is the value of the expression $4.7 \times 10^{-4} + 8.2 \times 10^{-6}$?

(A) 4.782×10^{-6}
(B) 4.782×10^{-4}
(C) 1.27×10^{-5}
(D) 1.27×10^{-7}

34. The equation of line m is $4x + 2y = 5$. What is the slope of a line that is perpendicular to line m?

(A) -2
(B) $-\frac{1}{2}$
(C) $\frac{1}{2}$
(D) 2

CONTINUE TO THE NEXT PAGE

35. A coin is flipped three times. The possible outcomes of landing on heads (H) and tails (T) are shown in the table below.

TTT	HHH
THT	HHT
TTH	HTT
THH	HTH

What is the probability that at least two of the tosses will land on heads?

(A) $\dfrac{1}{8}$

(B) $\dfrac{1}{4}$

(C) $\dfrac{1}{2}$

(D) $\dfrac{5}{8}$

36. A circle has a center with the coordinates $(-6, 1)$. A point on this circle has the coordinates $(2, 7)$. What is the radius of this circle?

(A) 4 grid units

(B) 5 grid units

(C) 6 grid units

(D) 10 grid units

37. Which describes all of the values of m that make the inequality $|3m + 2| > 4$ true?

(A) $m > \dfrac{2}{3}$

(B) $m < -2$

(C) $m > \dfrac{2}{3}$ or $m < -2$

(D) $m < -\dfrac{2}{3}$ or $m > 2$

CONTINUE TO THE NEXT PAGE

38. What is the result of $\begin{bmatrix} 4 & 5 \\ 1 & 7 \end{bmatrix} - \begin{bmatrix} 5 & 3 \\ 4 & 2 \end{bmatrix}$?

    (A) $\begin{bmatrix} -1 & 2 \\ 3 & 5 \end{bmatrix}$

    (B) $\begin{bmatrix} -1 & 2 \\ -3 & 5 \end{bmatrix}$

    (C) $\begin{bmatrix} 1 & 2 \\ 3 & 5 \end{bmatrix}$

    (D) $\begin{bmatrix} 1 & 2 \\ 3 & -5 \end{bmatrix}$

39. For all integers g and h, the operation $g \otimes h$ is defined by the equation $g \otimes h = g^2 - h^2$. Which answer choice has an odd value?

    (A) $17 \otimes 15$

    (B) $16 \otimes 15$

    (C) $16 \otimes 18$

    (D) $18 \otimes 16$

40. What is the solution set for $\dfrac{1}{2} \leq \dfrac{x+3}{4} \leq \dfrac{7}{8}$?

    (A) $-1 \leq x \leq \dfrac{1}{2}$

    (B) $\dfrac{1}{2} \leq x \leq 2$

    (C) $1 \leq x \leq 4$

    (D) $2 \leq x \leq 4$

41. Which graph represents the solution set for $7 \leq 4x - 1 \leq 19$?

(A)
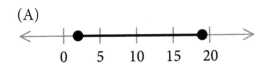

(B)
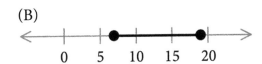

(C)
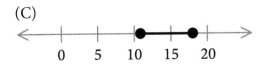

(D)
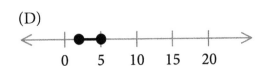

CONTINUE TO THE NEXT PAGE

42. X varies inversely with the square root of Y. If Y is multiplied by 9, then X is what fraction of its original value?

(A) $\dfrac{1}{81}$

(B) $\dfrac{1}{9}$

(C) $\dfrac{1}{3}$

(D) 3

43. There are 5,280 feet in one mile. If a car is moving at the speed of 40 miles per hour, how fast is it travelling in feet per second?

(A) $\dfrac{40 \times 5,280}{60}$

(B) $\dfrac{40 \times 60}{60 \times 5,280}$

(C) $\dfrac{40 \times 5,280 \times 60}{60}$

(D) $\dfrac{40 \times 5,280}{60 \times 60}$

44. Todd is going to flip a coin and then draw one marble from a bag that has two yellow marbles, three green marbles, and one blue marble. What is the probability that coin will land on heads and he will choose a green marble?

(A) $\dfrac{1}{6}$

(B) $\dfrac{1}{4}$

(C) $\dfrac{1}{3}$

(D) $\dfrac{2}{3}$

CONTINUE TO THE NEXT PAGE

45. In the equation $m = \frac{pq}{r}$, $p, q,$ and r are positive numbers. Which of the following statements is true?

    (A) If p is increased, then r will have to decrease if m is to remain constant.

    (B) If p is decreased, then r will have to increase if m is to remain constant.

    (C) If m is decreased, then r will have to decrease if p and q are to remain constant.

    (D) If m is increased, then r will have to decrease if p and q are to remain constant.

46. The first four terms of a sequence are shown below.

    $-1, 1, 3, 5$

    Which expression could be used to find the nth term in this sequence?

    (A) $n - 2$
    (B) $n + 2$
    (C) $2n - 3$
    (D) $3n - 4$

47. Lola is planning to take a survey to determine the most popular genre of books among the students in her school. Which sample of students would give her the most reliable information?

    (A) the students in the library club

    (B) a random sample of the students in her grade

    (C) a group of her friends

    (D) a random sample of students from the entire school

STOP

IF YOU HAVE TIME LEFT YOU MAY CHECK YOUR ANSWERS IN THIS SECTION ONLY

You will be given 30 minutes to plan and write an essay. The topic is printed on the next page. *Make sure that you write about this topic. Do NOT choose another topic.*

This essay gives you the chance to show your thinking and how well you can express your ideas. Do not worry about filling all of the space provided. The quality is more important than how much you write. You should write more than a brief paragraph, though.

A copy of this essay will be sent to the schools that you apply to. Make sure that you only write in the appropriate area on the answer sheet. Please print so that the admissions officers can understand what you wrote.

On the next page is the topic sheet. There is room on this sheet to make notes and collect your thoughts. The final essay should be written on the two lined sheets provided in the answer sheet, however. Make sure that you copy your topic at the top of the first lined page. Write only in blue or black ink.

Answer sheets are found near the beginning of this book.

REMINDER: Please remember to write the topic on the top of the first lined page in your answer sheet.

> If you were to spend a year studying only one subject, what would it be? Why would you choose to study that subject?

- Write only about this topic
- Only the lined sheets will be sent to schools
- Use only blue or black ink

Notes

_____

_____

_____

_____

_____

_____

_____

_____

_____

_____

_____

_____

_____

_____

_____

_____

_____

_____

Practice Test 2

Verbal Reasoning

40 questions
20 minutes

The Verbal Reasoning section has two parts. When you finish Part One, be sure to keep working on Part Two. For each answer that you choose, make sure to fill in the corresponding circle on the answer sheet.

Part One – Synonyms

Each question in Part One has a word in capital letters with four answer choices after it. Choose the answer choice with the word that comes closest in meaning to the word in capital letters.

SAMPLE QUESTION:

1.   SPEEDY:

    (A) loud
    (B) messy
    ● quick
    (D) small

Part Two – Sentence Completion

Each question in Part Two has a sentence with one or two blanks. Each blank takes the place of a word that is missing. The sentence has four answer choices after it. Choose the answer choice with the word or word pair that best completes the sentence.

SAMPLE QUESTION:

1.   Since the weather is getting warmer every day, it is particularly important to -------- more water.

    (A) create
    ● drink
    (C) leave
    (D) waste

STOP

DO NOT BEGIN THE SECTION UNTIL INSTRUCTED TO DO SO

Part One – Synonyms

Directions: Choose the word that is closest in meaning to the word that is in all capital letters.

1. PERSEVERANCE:

   (A) determination
   (B) fallacy
   (C) morale
   (D) solemnness

2. REPREHENSIBLE:

   (A) endearing
   (B) primary
   (C) shameful
   (D) timorous

3. FABRICATE:

   (A) abbreviate
   (B) concoct
   (C) reinforce
   (D) wring

4. VICINITY:

   (A) area
   (B) equipment
   (C) package
   (D) technique

5. VENTURE:

   (A) flood
   (B) inconvenience
   (C) greed
   (D) undertaking

6. ENVELOP:

   (A) grasp
   (B) launch
   (C) surround
   (D) tear

7. MORTIFY:

   (A) absorb
   (B) embarrass
   (C) jilt
   (D) reap

8. INSIPID:

   (A) dull
   (B) fatigued
   (C) normal
   (D) thrifty

9. ODIOUS:

   (A) familiar
   (B) genuine
   (C) horrible
   (D) scant

10. PATRON:

    (A) cadet
    (B) grade
    (C) praise
    (D) supporter

CONTINUE TO THE NEXT PAGE

11. NONCHALANT:

    (A) durable
    (B) interesting
    (C) resilient
    (D) unconcerned

12. ALLEVIATE:

    (A) assail
    (B) lighten
    (C) retrieve
    (D) thwart

13. FRANK:

    (A) blunt
    (B) dignified
    (C) needy
    (D) tricky

14. RECEPTACLE:

    (A) appliance
    (B) container
    (C) pact
    (D) substitute

15. MIRTH:

    (A) dread
    (B) faith
    (C) laughter
    (D) thrill

16. SCATHING:

    (A) biting
    (B) capable
    (C) precious
    (D) tight

17. SOLACE:

    (A) alibi
    (B) comfort
    (C) glimpse
    (D) movement

18. PLACATE:

    (A) appease
    (B) delve
    (C) ostracize
    (D) sacrifice

19. LAUDABLE:

    (A) cartoonish
    (B) feeble
    (C) hushed
    (D) praiseworthy

CONTINUE TO THE NEXT PAGE

Part Two – Sentence Completion

Directions: Choose the word or word pair that best completes the sentence.

20. Since it is hard to count every single person in a country, it is impossible to -------- an exact figure for the number of people unemployed.

    (A) accede
    (B) languish
    (C) permeate
    (D) tabulate

21. Ethanol is a controversial fuel that has been -------- as both the savior of the environment and a potential cause of widespread hunger.

    (A) characterized
    (B) criticized
    (C) encouraged
    (D) sanctioned

22. While attending theater performances is considered a highly respectable pastime today, during colonial times it was considered downright -------- to attend a play.

    (A) creative
    (B) indecent
    (C) luxurious
    (D) resourceful

23. While there have been many reported sightings of the Eastern mountain lion, the animal is so -------- that few scientists are willing to say that it even still exists for certain.

    (A) elusive
    (B) imaginary
    (C) nonchalant
    (D) sheltered

CONTINUE TO THE NEXT PAGE

24. When Copernicus announced that the Earth revolved around the sun, there was an enormous -------- between people who agreed with Copernicus and those who were convinced the sun revolved around the Earth.

   (A) adulation
   (B) pageant
   (C) schism
   (D) transformation

25. The butterfly effect is the theory that even a(n) -------- change in one place can lead to major changes in another place.

   (A) familiar
   (B) laborious
   (C) planned
   (D) slight

26. Author Jane Austen never received the -------- she deserved during her lifetime because her novels were initially published anonymously.

   (A) acclaim
   (B) fables
   (C) livelihood
   (D) treachery

27. Starting a new business is nerve-wracking since there is no -------- that it will succeed.

   (A) component
   (B) guarantee
   (C) intention
   (D) specification

CONTINUE TO THE NEXT PAGE

28. It is tough to ignore the -------- evidence that seatbelts make cars safer for both the driver and the passengers.

   (A) considerable
   (B) dwindling
   (C) offensive
   (D) ponderous

29. The landscape of the Sahara is so -------- that few species can survive there.

   (A) adventurous
   (B) desolate
   (C) secret
   (D) weary

30. The -------- odor of some cheeses often discourages children from tasting them.

   (A) assimiliated
   (B) helpful
   (C) pungent
   (D) sensible

31. At the 1934 World's Fair, visitors could purchase a glass lantern -------- to take home as a memento of their visit to the fair.

   (A) carriage
   (B) journey
   (C) mainstay
   (D) souvenir

32. Because our plans were --------, I was not surprised to see that they had been -------- from the calendar.

   (A) irritable . . . refreshed
   (B) lucid . . . removed
   (C) pragmatic . . . misunderstood
   (D) tentative . . . expunged

CONTINUE TO THE NEXT PAGE

33. While it now seems perfectly -------- that the head of a government should be elected by the people, even just a couple of hundred years ago that -------- was revolutionary.

    (A) anachronistic ... formation
    (B) commonplace ... concept
    (C) eminent ... lineage
    (D) mediocre ... lore

34. Artist Salvador Dali was so -------- that his outrageous behavior sometimes -------- his artistic achievements.

    (A) eccentric ... overshadowed
    (B) favorable ... upheld
    (C) severe ... galvanized
    (D) virtuous ... spurred

35. Despite -------- from neighbors who lived next to the old railroad bed, a bike trail was -------- where the train used to run.

    (A) divisions ... banned
    (B) endorsements ... designed
    (C) interest ... paved
    (D) objections ... created

36. During the Middle Ages, Venice became a center of -------- and therefore merchants were highly -------- in society.

    (A) action ... noticed
    (B) commerce ... regarded
    (C) immigration ... fatigued
    (D) privacy ... overlooked

CONTINUE TO THE NEXT PAGE

37. Although carnivorous plants are --------, the Venus flytrap and Cape sundew species are proof that it is not a(n) -------- that some plants can eat insects.

    (A) familiar . . . decision
    (B) irritating . . . minority
    (C) occasional . . . truth
    (D) rare . . . fabrication

38. Athletes often exercise for extended periods of time in order to build -------- but the risk is that -------- could result from overstrained muscles.

    (A) belligerence . . . rest
    (B) endurance . . . strength
    (C) stamina . . . injury
    (D) transformations . . . reflexes

39. In order to provide more privacy, the -------- glass was etched to create a more -------- surface.

    (A) clouded . . . permeable
    (B) lavish . . . murky
    (C) responsible . . . secretive
    (D) transparent . . . opaque

40. Some cicadas, a type of insect, can remain -------- for seventeen years by -------- underground as newly hatched nymphs and remaining inactive.

    (A) dormant . . . burrowing
    (B) feverish . . . dispensing
    (C) obsolete . . . prowling
    (D) subdued . . . synchronizing

STOP

IF YOU HAVE TIME LEFT YOU MAY CHECK YOUR ANSWERS IN THIS SECTION ONLY

Quantitative Reasoning

37 questions

35 minutes

Each math question has four answer choices after it. Choose the answer choice that best answers the question.

Make sure that you fill in the correct answer on your answer sheet. You may write in the test booklet.

SAMPLE QUESTION:

1. What is the perimeter of a rectangle that has a length of 3 cm and a width of 5 cm?
    $(P = 2l + 2w)$

    (A) 6 cm

    (B) 10 cm

    (C) 8 cm

    ● 16 cm

The correct answer is 16 cm and circle D is filled in.

STOP

DO NOT BEGIN THE SECTION UNTIL INSTRUCTED TO DO SO

Part One – Word Problems

1. If $m - n = 4$, then which expression is equal to n?

   (A) $m - 4$

   (B) $m + 4$

   (C) $-m - 4$

   (D) $4 - m$

2. Victoria has had 7 science tests this semester. She figured out that the range of her scores was 9 points, the median of her test scores was 83, and the mean of her test scores was 84. Now she can only find 5 of the tests and her scores on these tests are 81, 81, 83, 85, and 86. What are the scores on the two missing tests?

   (A) 81 and 90

   (B) 82 and 89

   (C) 82 and 90

   (D) 83 and 89

3. What is the value of the expression $2 + \frac{2}{3}$?

   (A) $\frac{4}{3}$

   (B) $\frac{5}{3}$

   (C) $2.\overline{6}$

   (D) 2.666666667

4. If q is a multiple of m and m is a factor of r, which statement must be true?

   (A) q is a factor of r

   (B) r is a multiple of q

   (C) the least common factor of q and r is m

   (D) m is a factor of qr

CONTINUE TO THE NEXT PAGE

5.   A net is shown below that is to be folded into a cube.

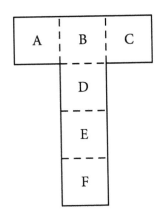

If this net is folded into a cube such that side E is on the bottom, what side will be on top?

(A)   A

(B)   B

(C)   D

(D)   F

6.   The figure below is a cube.

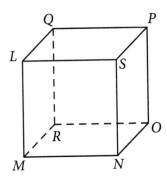

If the following segments were drawn in, which would be the longest?

(A) $\overline{MN}$

(B) $\overline{MO}$

(C) $\overline{MQ}$

(D) $\overline{MP}$

CONTINUE TO THE NEXT PAGE

7. If the greatest of three consecutive odd integers is three more than twice the least integer, which equation could be used to solve for the three integers if x represents the least integer?

    (A) $2x + 3 = x + 2$
    (B) $2x = 3(x + 2)$
    (C) $2x + 3 = x + 4$
    (D) $2(x + 4) = x + 3$

8. If $(x + b)^2 = x^2 + 12x + 36$, then what is the value of b?

    (A) 3
    (B) 4
    (C) 6
    (D) 18

9. If the length of a rectangle is increased by 30% and the width is decreased by 30%, then what will be the effect on the area?

    (A) it will increase
    (B) it will stay the same
    (C) it will decrease
    (D) cannot be determined

CONTINUE TO THE NEXT PAGE

10. Kate left school and started to walk home before remembering a book that she needed to bring home. She stopped, looked through her book bag, found the book, and continued walking home. The graph below shows her distance from school as a function of time.

Kate's distance from school

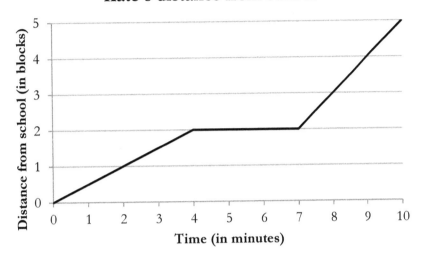

How far was Kate from the school, in blocks, when she stopped to look in her bag?

(A) 2

(B) 3

(C) 4

(D) 7

CONTINUE TO THE NEXT PAGE

11. The graph below shows the number of siblings for each of the children in Ms. Jackson's class.

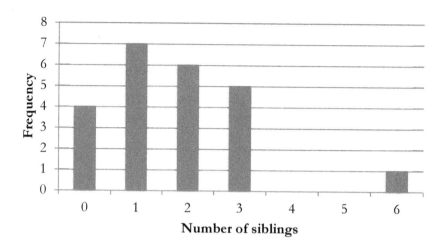

What is the median of this data?

(A) 1
(B) 2
(C) 3
(D) 4

12. If $m + n = 15$ and $m - n = 3$, then what is the value of $m^2 - n^2$?

(A) 12
(B) 45
(C) 90
(D) 216

CONTINUE TO THE NEXT PAGE

13. The stem-and-leaf plot below shows the scores on a history test.

6	3 4 5 5 7 8
7	2 2 4 6 7 8 8
8	1 1 1 5 6 6 7 7 8 8
9	2 2 3 6 8 8
10	0 0

What is the mode of this data?

(A) 8

(B) 72

(C) 81

(D) 92

14. Which regular polygon would have the greatest interior angle measure?

(A) triangle

(B) square

(C) hexagon

(D) octagon

15. If $b - c = 3$ and $b^2 + bc + c^2 = 39$, then what is the value of $b^3 - c^3$?

(A) 36

(B) 42

(C) 78

(D) 117

CONTINUE TO THE NEXT PAGE

16. There are red, white, and yellow flowers in a bouquet. If a flower is chosen at random, the probability that the flower will be red is $\frac{3}{7}$ and the probability that the flower will be white is $\frac{2}{7}$. Which piece of information would NOT be sufficient for figuring out how many yellow flowers are in the bouquet?

    (A)   the probability of choosing a yellow flower
    (B)   the total number of flowers
    (C)   the number of red flowers
    (D)   the number of white flowers

17. A rectangle has a perimeter of 20 centimeters. If the length and the width are both measured in whole centimeters, what is the greatest possible area of the rectangle?

    (A)   9 cm²
    (B)   16 cm²
    (C)   20 cm²
    (D)   25 cm²

18. A bowl contains 4 white marbles, 3 green marbles, 6 blue marbles, and 5 black marbles. One marble is drawn, then placed back in the bag, and a second marble is chosen. What is the probability that both marbles are blue?

    (A) $\frac{1}{9}$

    (B) $\frac{1}{6}$

    (C) $\frac{1}{3}$

    (D) $\frac{2}{3}$

CONTINUE TO THE NEXT PAGE

19. Della is conducting a survey about who people will vote for in the next town election. Which sample will give Della the most relevant data to predict the winner of the election?

    (A) a random sample of citizens in her town

    (B) her friends

    (C) the people who campaign for each candidate

    (D) a random sample of citizens who are eligible to vote in her town

20. If $\frac{q}{r} = \frac{2}{3}$, then which expression must also be equal to $\frac{2}{3}$ if q and r are both positive?

    (A) $\frac{q+2}{r+3}$

    (B) $\frac{q-2}{r-3}$

    (C) $\frac{2q}{3r}$

    (D) $\frac{3q}{2r}$

Part Two – Quantitative Comparisons

Directions: Use the information in the question to compare the quantities in Columns A and B. After comparing the two quantities, choose the correct answer choice:

    (A) Quantity in Column A is greater.
    (B) Quantity in Column B is greater.
    (C) The quantities in Column A and Column B are equal.
    (D) Cannot be determined from information given.

Column A	**Column B**
21. $\dfrac{2}{3 + \frac{3}{4}}$	$\dfrac{2}{3 + 4}$

CONTINUE TO THE NEXT PAGE

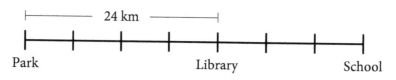

Park   Library   School

	Column A	**Column B**
22.	Distance from the library to the school	20 km

Pedro received the scores of 82, 82, 85, and 88 on four tests.

	Column A	**Column B**
23.	85	The mean of Pedro's test scores

$$V = \frac{1}{3}\pi r^2 h$$

	Column A	**Column B**
24.	$\dfrac{3V}{\pi h}$	r

The product of 4 consecutive integers is 120.

	Column A	**Column B**
25.	The smallest of the integers	9

For all real numbers x and y, $x \blacksquare y$ is defined by $x \blacksquare y = x^2 + 2xy + y^2$.

	Column A	**Column B**
26.	$3 \blacksquare 4$	$4 \blacksquare 3$

CONTINUE TO THE NEXT PAGE

Lola's scores on her first five tests were 82, 86, 90, 92, and 94. Lola has one more test to take and wants to receive a final average score of 90.

	Column A	**Column B**
27.	92	The minimum score that Lola could receive on her 6th test and have an average score of 90

The equation of line p is $3x + 2y = 6$. Line r is parallel to line p.

	Column A	**Column B**
28.	The slope of line r	$-\dfrac{3}{2}$

y is any real number.

	Column A	**Column B**
29.	y^2	$\dfrac{1}{y^{-2}}$

$$3x + 2 > 4x$$

	Column A	**Column B**
30.	0	x

	Column A	**Column B**
31.	40% of 50	25% of 80

CONTINUE TO THE NEXT PAGE

The histogram below shows the test scores of students in a science class.

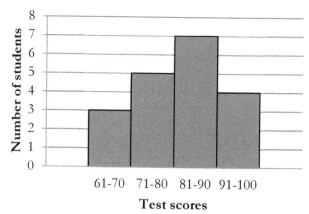

	Column A	Column B
32.	The mean score	The range of scores

	Column A	Column B
33.	$\sqrt{90}$	9

$$a < b < 0 < c$$

	Column A	Column B
34.	$a + b$	c

A bag contains green, blue, and red marbles. A marble is to be randomly selected from the bag.

	Column A	Column B
35.	The probability of choosing a green marble	The probability of choosing a blue marble

CONTINUE TO THE NEXT PAGE

The graph below shows the annual budget of the Stevenson family. They spend $60,000 a year.

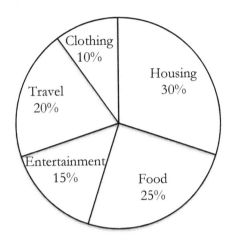

Column A	**Column B**
36. Dollar amount spent on food	Dollar amount spent on entertainment and clothing combined

Triangle A   Triangle B

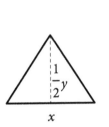 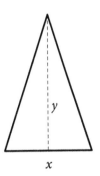

Column A	**Column B**
37. Area of triangle A	$\frac{1}{2}$ area of triangle B

STOP

IF YOU HAVE TIME LEFT YOU MAY CHECK YOUR ANSWERS IN THIS SECTION ONLY

Reading Comprehension

36 questions
35 minutes

The Reading Comprehension section has six short passages. Each passage has six questions after it. For each question, choose the answer choice that comes closest to what is stated or implied in the passage. You may write in the test booklet.

STOP

DO NOT BEGIN THE SECTION UNTIL INSTRUCTED TO DO SO

Questions #1-6

1   By all accounts, Hedy Lamarr was a stunningly beautiful actress. She was famous
2   for her glamorous looks, her exotic accent, and her willingness to play parts that were
3   considered risqué in the 1930s and 1940s. Few people know that she held a patent for
4   frequency hopping technology, which became the basis for the wireless life that we now
5   lead. We can thank a siren of the silver screen for technologies such as Bluetooth and
6   Wi-Fi network connections.

7   Hedy Lamarr was born in Austria-Hungary and acted in her first film at age 18.
8   She caught the eye of Friedrich Mandl, a very wealthy Austrian who produced weapons
9   and ammunition, and they were married when she was just 19 years old. Mandl was
10   incredibly controlling and insisted that Lamarr accompany him to business meetings
11   where he discussed military technology with rulers such as Hitler and Mussolini. He
12   brought her along as merely a pretty wife, but she left with knowledge of applied science
13   and how weapons were designed.

14   Marriage to Mandl proved intolerable, and Lamarr to fled to Paris. She met Louis
15   B. Mayer, a famous film producer. He brought her to Hollywood and made her a star.
16   She played the exotic seductress opposite many of the leading men of the 1940s.

17   In her off hours, however, she was busy designing inventions. She spent time with
18   a neighbor, composer George Antheil, who was writing pieces that used multiple player
19   pianos at the same time. During this time, World War II was raging on and Lamarr and
20   Antheil discussed the fact that radio-controlled torpedoes were important to the war
21   effort but highly susceptible to being thrown off course by broadcasting interference.
22   She used the knowledge she had gained during her marriage to Mandl to develop the
23   idea of using torpedoes that hopped frequencies so that the enemy could not hit upon
24   the right frequency and divert the torpedo. Together, Lamarr and Antheil created a
25   system using a piano roll so that a torpedo and a control center could have a matching
26   pattern of frequency changes that would be impossible to crack.

27   In 1942, Lamarr and Antheil received a patent for this new technology, and they
28   took it to the U.S. Navy. Rather than being interested in Lamarr's new invention, they
29   encouraged her to put it aside and use her celebrity status to sell war bonds instead. It
30   wasn't until 1962 that the Navy appreciated the genius of her and Antheil's system and
31   employed it in a blockade of Cuba. The seemingly simple invention of using a piano
32   roll to change frequencies became the basis for modern spread-spectrum technology. It
33   is this technology that allows wireless networks to operate, making the internet available
34   to people all over the globe.

CONTINUE TO THE NEXT PAGE

1. Which best expresses the main idea of this passage?

   (A) Hedy Lamarr is an actress best known for her sultry roles.
   (B) Our lives were changed by a technology developed by a woman better known for her movie roles.
   (C) Hedy Lamarr's invention changed the course of World War II.
   (D) Hedy Lamarr and George Antheil had an unusual partnership.

2. The passages states that Lamarr left her marriage to Friedrich Mandl with

   (A) a large financial settlement.
   (B) important business contacts.
   (C) a movie contract.
   (D) knowledge of weapons systems.

3. According to the passage, how did Lamarr and Antheil's system prevent torpedoes from being diverted by the enemy?

   (A) Unpredictable changes in frequency made it almost impossible for the enemy to create broadcast interference.
   (B) The system created broadcast interference for the enemy's signal.
   (C) Their system allowed torpedoes to emit their own frequencies.
   (D) They created a torpedo that did not rely on radio-controlled frequencies.

4. In line 24, the word "divert" most nearly means

   (A) limit.
   (B) signal to.
   (C) turn away.
   (D) eliminate.

5. The second paragraph (lines 7-13) states that young Hedy Lamarr did all of the following EXCEPT

   (A) marry a wealthy Austrian man.
   (B) act in films.
   (C) attend meetings where Mussolini was present.
   (D) discuss weapons with Hitler.

6. The purpose of the last sentence (lines 32-34) is to

   (A) explain how the internet works.
   (B) describe a system that has never been implemented.
   (C) illustrate the importance of Lamarr and Antheil's invention.
   (D) disprove an earlier thesis.

CONTINUE TO THE NEXT PAGE

Questions #7-12

This passage is adapted from Everyday Mysteries: Fun Science Facts from the Library of Congress.

1   Many children have attempted to fry an egg on a hot sidewalk and wound up with
2 a sloppy mess instead of a fried egg.
3   An egg needs a temperature of 158°F to become firm. In order to cook, proteins
4 in the egg must denature (modify), then coagulate, and that won't happen until the
5 temperature rises enough to start and maintain the process.
6   The sidewalk presents several challenges to this. According to an experiment
7 reported by Robert Wolke, sidewalk temperatures can vary depending on the
8 composition of the sidewalk, whether it is in direct sunlight, and of course, the air
9 temperature. Dark objects absorb more light, so blacktop paving would be hotter than
10 concrete. More often than not, sidewalks are concrete. Wolke found that a hot sidewalk
11 might only get up to 145°F. Once you crack the egg onto the sidewalk, the egg cools the
12 sidewalk slightly. Pavement of any kind is a poor conductor of heat, so lacking an
13 additional heat source from below or from the side, the egg will not cook evenly.
14   Something closer to the conditions of a frying pan would be the hood of a car.
15 Metal conducts heat better and gets hotter, so people actually have been able to cook an
16 egg on a car hood's surface.
17   Still, the idea of cooking an egg on a sidewalk won't die. It is so intriguing that the
18 city of Oatman, Arizona, hosts an annual Solar Egg Frying Contest on the 4th of July.
19 Contestants get 15 minutes to make an attempt using solar (sun) power alone. Oatman
20 judges, however, do allow some aids, such as mirrors, aluminum reflectors, or
21 magnifying glasses, which would help to focus the heat onto the egg itself. It turns out
22 that eggs also have a bit of an advantage in Arizona, the land of low humidity and high
23 heat. Liquids evaporate rapidly when humidity is low. The eggs have a bit of "help"
24 while they cook, and they dry out faster.

7.   The primary purpose of this passage is to

   (A)   describe the conditions that allow an egg to be cooked on the sidewalk.
   (B)   provide the scientific basis for a particular phenomenon.
   (C)   explain why children think that you can fry an egg on the sidewalk.
   (D)   present the findings of Robert Wolke.

CONTINUE TO THE NEXT PAGE

8. In line 4, the word "coagulate" most nearly means

    (A) thicken.
    (B) dissolve.
    (C) change.
    (D) stop.

9. In the last paragraph (lines 17-24), the author implies that for an egg to cook

    (A) some of the liquid must evaporate.
    (B) magnifying glasses have to be used.
    (C) the sun must be bright.
    (D) a pan has to be used.

10. The author states that once an egg is cracked onto a sidewalk, the temperature of the sidewalk cools slightly because

    (A) it is a dark color.
    (B) the egg does not cook evenly.
    (C) the egg blocks some of the sunlight.
    (D) concrete does not conduct heat well.

11. It can be inferred from the passage that frying an egg on the hood of a black car would

    (A) not be possible.
    (B) require the use of other aids such as mirrors and reflectors.
    (C) be easier than frying an egg on the hood of a white car.
    (D) be harder than frying an egg on blacktop pavement.

12. The author does all of the following EXCEPT

    (A) present research.
    (B) describe a process.
    (C) quote from an authoritative source.
    (D) present an illustration.

CONTINUE TO THE NEXT PAGE

Questions #13-18

1   Visitors who ventured to the Uribante Reservoir in Táchira, Venezuela, between
2   1985 and 2010 were greeted by an unnerving sight: in the middle of the reservoir, an old
3   and rotting cross rose from the waters. This cross had not been planted in the center of
4   a body of water, but rather it was all that remained visible of a town that was flooded
5   when a hydroelectric dam was built.
6   In 1985, Potosi was a town of 1,200 inhabitants located in the Andes Mountains.
7   One day, the then-president of Venezuela, Carlos Andrés Pérez, flew in by helicopter
8   and declared that the entire town would be flooded and that all residents must be
9   evacuated and relocated. According to one resident, Josefa Garcia, "he said we'd all be
10   expropriated and we had to leave. It took away our hope." True to the president's
11   words, the hydroelectric dam was built and the town was flooded, leaving only the
12   church spire as evidence of what once had existed on that site.
13   In 2008, however, more and more of the spire began to be revealed. Due to the El
14   Niño weather pattern, a drought had come to Venezuela. By 2010, the water had
15   receded almost completely, and the town of Petosi emerged once again. The church
16   building that had supported that spire for so many years surfaced, although only the
17   façade of the church remained after being underwater for 26 years. The church
18   graveyard, ruins of old houses, and the outline of the town square were revealed as the
19   drought deepened and the surface of the reservoir sunk lower. Josefa Garcia was once
20   again able to walk through the churchyard where she had worked for many years and
21   attended mass for more. With a heavy heart, she commented, "It brings me joy, but it
22   also makes me sad to see the situation that we are in."

13. This passage is primarily concerned with

(A) explaining the tough choices that must be made to produce electricity.
(B) criticizing Carlos Andres Perez's decision to flood Potosi.
(C) exploring what life was like in Potosi before the dam was built.
(D) describing the experience of one town.

14. Josefa Garcia's tone in the last sentence (lines 21-22) can best be described as

(A) angry.
(B) conflicted.
(C) subdued.
(D) tense.

CONTINUE TO THE NEXT PAGE

15. The passage implies that the residents of Potosi

    (A) opposed the dam project.
    (B) had mixed feelings about the dam being built.
    (C) were not asked about the dam.
    (D) supported President Carlos Andrés Pérez.

16. In line 2, the word "unnerving" most nearly means

    (A) uncommon.
    (B) understood.
    (C) unreliable.
    (D) unsettling.

17. When Josefa Garcia states, "it also makes me sad to see the situation that we are in," she is most likely referring to

    (A) the drought that caused the waters to recede.
    (B) the flooding of the town.
    (C) Venezuela's political situation.
    (D) her own failing health.

18. It can be inferred from the passage that the El Niño weather pattern

    (A) occurs every year.
    (B) causes unusual weather conditions.
    (C) often leads to heavy rains.
    (D) is helpful for farmers.

CONTINUE TO THE NEXT PAGE

Questions #19-24

The following passage is from Newspaper Death Watch: Chronicling the Decline of Newspapers and the Rebirth of Journalism. It is written by Paul Gillin, a journalist.

1   On one level we can understand the teeth-gnashing that followed the Associated
2   Press' announcement that it plans to start using robots to write the majority of corporate
3   earnings stories. Robots seem to bring out the Luddite in all of us. What we can't
4   understand is why anyone outside of a few shop stewards want to preserve the jobs that
5   will invariably be lost to this new kind of automation.
6   Actually, the AP says no jobs will be eliminated. "This is about using technology
7   to free journalists to do more journalism and less data processing, not about eliminating
8   jobs," wrote Lou Farrara, vice president and managing editor, on the AP blog. You can
9   bet that robots are going to eliminate reporting jobs in the future, though, just like
10   linotype machines replaced human typesetters and computer pagination replaced paste-
11   up jobs. It's called efficiency, and job loss is one of the distasteful consequences.
12   We'd suggest that much of the labor impact will actually be felt overseas, which is
13   where the menial jobs have already migrated. Robo-journalists in India and the
14   Philippines will need to improve their skills to continue to get work from U.S. and
15   European publishers, and journalists in home offices will need to up their games as well.
16   That's a good thing.
17   What isn't good is preserving jobs that eat up time and the editor's attention. In
18   one of our recent assignments we worked with a technology news site that employs a
19   small staff of seasoned journalists but that gets most of its content from an offshore body
20   shop that rewrites press releases and news from other websites. The reporters who write
21   this chum make about five cents a word, and in our view they're overpaid.
22   Stories come in full of grammatical and usage errors, and many are missing basic
23   facts or explanations. Professional editors spend hours each day fixing these mistakes
24   and trying to educate the writers, which is a fool's errand because most of them don't
25   last more than a few months on the job anyway. These tasks can now be automated,
26   and many of them will be. The result will be a better quality of work for everyone
27   involved.

---

19.   The primary purpose of this passage is to

(A)   praise the work of robo-journalists who free up the editor's time for more
      important tasks.
(B)   describe the effect of robots on the overseas labor market.
(C)   suggest that rather than destroying journalism, robots will actually
      improve journalism's current state.
(D)   take issue with a decision made the Associated Press.

CONTINUE TO THE NEXT PAGE

20. The writer's attitude toward automation can best be described as

   (A) disdainful.
   (B) encouraging.
   (C) indifferent.
   (D) stumped.

21. In line 19, the word "seasoned" most nearly means

   (A) experienced.
   (B) speedy.
   (C) uneducated.
   (D) varied.

22. The purpose of the final paragraph (lines 22-27) is to

   (A) explain how robo-journalists are used.
   (B) lament the decline of journalism.
   (C) give an example of research that supports the author's main point.
   (D) illustrate how using material written by a computer, and not a person, could save time for editors.

23. According the passage, the public reaction to the Associate Press' decision to use robots was

   (A) an immediate call for banning stories written by robots.
   (B) characterized by anxiety.
   (C) generally supportive.
   (D) ambivalent.

24. In lines 6-8, Lou Farrara says that jobs will not be eliminated because

   (A) the hours that are eliminated for data processing will be made up for with increased time spent on journalism.
   (B) operations that were moved overseas will return to the United States.
   (C) there will be a reduction in the number of outside writers used.
   (D) an increase in newspaper sales will allow operations to expand.

CONTINUE TO THE NEXT PAGE

Questions #25-30

1   The development of a prosperous society is often not due to great leaders or
2 specific policies, but rather it comes from the development of a new technology in the
3 right place at the right time. Such was the case for the Republic of Venice during the
4 Middle Ages. The Venetian Arsenal, and the revolutionary production processes
5 pioneered there, led Venice into a period of dominance.
6   While the exact date that the Arsenal was built has not been determined, operations
7 were in full swing by the 13th century BCE. It was the largest industrial complex in Europe,
8 covering about 15% of the land in Venice and employing an estimated 16,000 people at
9 its height. The Arsenal consisted of a heavily armed compound surrounded by two miles
10 of ramparts. Within this huge complex, the various parts of ships were fabricated in
11 different areas. These parts could then be assembled into a ship in an assembly line that
12 was aided by a canal. The ship would move along the canal, and specialized teams would
13 add in the parts that had been made in other areas of the Arsenal. Assembly line
14 production allowed a ship to be put together in as little a one day, whereas in other parts
15 of Europe it could take months to build a ship.
16   With this new technology came an influx of power. Venice's location on the water,
17 combined with assembly line production of ships, allowed the Venetian navy to
18 dominate the Mediterranean Sea, which was a vital trade route in the Middle Ages.
19 There arose a social class referred to as the arsenalotti that consisted of tradesmen who
20 worked within the Arsenal. An unusually close relationship formed between the
21 patrician families that had ruled Venice for generations and the working class
22 arsenalotti. It was a case of a mutually beneficial relationship – the arsenalotti could
23 advance the pet projects of the ruling class, and in return the arsenalotti received social
24 stature that most working class citizens could only dream of. Assembly line production
25 had not only built the Republic of Venice into a formidable naval power, it also shook
26 up the entire social class system.

---

25. Which best describes the main idea of this passage?

   (A) Venice was a place of rapid growth in the Middle Ages.
   (B) Shipbuilding has been improved upon many times in the past.
   (C) The arsenalotti became too powerful.
   (D) A technological advance can have far reaching consequences.

CONTINUE TO THE NEXT PAGE

26. According to the passage, the patrician families of Venice befriended the arsenalotti because the arsenalotti

    (A) were newly wealthy.
    (B) controlled work being done in the Arsenal.
    (C) took over as the ruling class of Venice.
    (D) wouldn't share their new technology.

27. The author suggests that Venice came to dominate Mediterranean trade because

    (A) of the breakdown of social structure in Venice.
    (B) other European countries were distracted by conflicts.
    (C) the Venetian Arsenal built ships much faster than other countries could.
    (D) there were many skilled shipbuilders in Venice.

28. The author most likely mentions that the Arsenal covered 15% of the land in Venice and employed 16,000 people in order to

    (A) give the reader a sense of how important the Arsenal became in Venice.
    (B) provide a contrast to other ship building sites in Europe.
    (C) praise the Venetian people for creating such a compound.
    (D) establish a timeline for the creation of the Arsenal.

29. In lines 23-24, the author implies that members of the working class

    (A) experienced great upheaval with the creation of the Arsenal.
    (B) could rarely advance their social standings.
    (C) socialized frequently with the ruling class.
    (D) moved frequently.

30. The passage suggests that using specialized teams

    (A) reduced the cost of building a ship.
    (B) increased worker satisfaction.
    (C) led to the creation of the Arsenal.
    (D) decreased the amount of time it took to build a ship.

CONTINUE TO THE NEXT PAGE

Questions #31-36

The following passage is adapted from a narrative collected by the Writers' Project in 1939.

1   The Luellings brought the first cherry trees to Oregon. Henderson it was, who
2 took the initial step in bringing that first good variety of grafted fruit trees. The details
3 of this story are interesting. Henderson, planning to come to Oregon in the spring of
4 1846, secured the cooperation of a neighbor, named John Fisher, for his plan.
5   First, they procured a stout wagon, then they made two boxes, 12 inches deep and
6 of sufficient length and breadth that when placed in the wagon-box, side by side, they
7 filled it completely. The boxes were then filled with a compost, or soil, consisting
8 principally of charcoal and earth, and in this 700 small trees were planted. The trees
9 were from 20 inches to four feet high, protected by light strong strips of hickory bolted
10 on to posts, set in staples on the wagon box. For that wagon alone three yoke of oxen
11 were detailed. Can't you see those men working and planning to the utmost detail, that
12 Oregon might have in time the wonderful cherries and other fruit for which it is now
13 famous? And there are those today who dare to say the pioneers had no vision, that they
14 were mere adventurers.
15   Well, to go on with our story. The Luelling caravan consisted of many wagons:
16 one for the Luellings, one for the Fisher family, two for Nathan Hockett's family, and
17 the Nursery Wagon itself — seven wagons in all. The caravan started its long journey
18 across the plains, on April 17, 1846. It traveled about fifteen miles a day, and every day,
19 no matter how scarce the water, nor how far the distance between watered camps, each
20 and every one of those little 700 trees were carefully sprinkled with water.

---

31.   The primary purpose of this passage is to

(A)   relate the difficulties that early pioneers encountered.
(B)   explain the importance of perseverance.
(C)   tell the story of how cherry trees came to Oregon.
(D)   provide background information about the founding of Oregon.

32.   The tone of this passage can best be described as

(A)   critical.
(B)   informative.
(C)   optimistic.
(D)   nostalgic.

CONTINUE TO THE NEXT PAGE

33. The passage suggests that some early settlers were criticized for

    (A) being motivated only by a sense of adventure.
    (B) not planning well for travel.
    (C) not taking enough water for the journey.
    (D) forming caravans that were too large.

34. In line 5, the word "procured" most nearly means

    (A) cleaned.
    (B) launched.
    (C) obtained.
    (D) rejected.

35. It can be inferred from the passage that Henderson Luelling and John Fisher

    (A) frequently took long trips with their families.
    (B) knew a fair amount about fruit trees.
    (C) were on a very limited budget.
    (D) brought an assortment of different types of cherry trees.

36. The final sentence (lines 18-20) is included in order to

    (A) emphasize the personal sacrifice that one group made to bring cherries to Oregon.
    (B) suggest that bringing cherry trees to Oregon was not worth the effort.
    (C) provide a satisfying conclusion to the story.
    (D) spark a discussion about the importance of agriculture.

STOP

IF YOU HAVE TIME LEFT YOU MAY CHECK YOUR ANSWERS IN THIS SECTION ONLY

Mathematics Achievement

47 questions
40 minutes

Each math question has four answer choices after it. Choose the answer choice that best answers the question.

Make sure that you fill in the correct answer on your answer sheet. You may write in the test booklet.

SAMPLE QUESTION:

1. Which number can be divided by 4 with nothing left over?

    (A) 6
    ● 12
    (C) 15
    (D) 22

Since 12 can be divided by 4 with no remainder, circle B is filled in.

STOP

DO NOT BEGIN THE SECTION UNTIL INSTRUCTED TO DO SO

1. If p and q are both irrational numbers, then the result of $p + q$ could NOT be

   (A) an irrational number
   (B) an integer
   (C) a complex number
   (D) a rational number

2. Triangle ABC is similar to triangle DEF. The length of $\overline{AB}$ is 4 cm and the length of $\overline{BC}$ is 6 cm. If the length of $\overline{DE}$ is 6 cm, then what is the length of $\overline{EF}$?

   (A) 2 cm
   (B) 4 cm
   (C) 6 cm
   (D) 9 cm

3. Which expression is equivalent to $5a^3b^2 - (4a^2b^3 - 2a^3b^2) + 2a^2b^3$

   (A) a^3b^2
   (B) $5a^3b^2$
   (C) $3a^3b^2 - 2a^2b^3$
   (D) $7a^3b^2 - 2a^2b^3$

4. Andrea has taken six tests. On the first five tests she received scores of 84, 90, 81, 88, and 70. If her median test score is 85, what score did she receive on the sixth test?

   (A) 82
   (B) 84
   (C) 85
   (D) 86

CONTINUE TO THE NEXT PAGE

5.   Triangle GHI is shown below. The length of $\overline{GH}$ is 3 and the length of $\overline{GI}$ is 4.

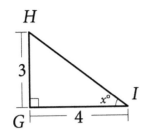

Which of the following is equal to $\sin x°$?

(A) $\dfrac{3}{5}$

(B) $\dfrac{3}{4}$

(C) $\dfrac{4}{5}$

(D) $\dfrac{4}{3}$

6.   What value(s) of x make $\dfrac{(x-2)(x+3)}{x^2-4}$ equal to zero?

(A) $x = 2$ only

(B) $x = -3$ only

(C) $x = 2$ or $x = 3$

(D) $x = 2$ or $x = -3$

7.   One of the angles is given in the parallelogram below.

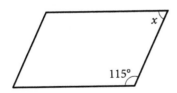

What is the value of x?

(A) 65°

(B) 85°

(C) 130°

(D) 245°

CONTINUE TO THE NEXT PAGE

8. If $2(4m - 3) = mn - 6$, then what is the value of n?

   (A) 3
   (B) 4
   (C) 8
   (D) 16

9. A triangle has side lengths of 3 and 10. Which of the following could be the length of the third side?

   (A) 7
   (B) 8
   (C) 13
   (D) 14

10. For a diving competition, there are six judges. The graph below shows the scores that a diver received on a single dive.

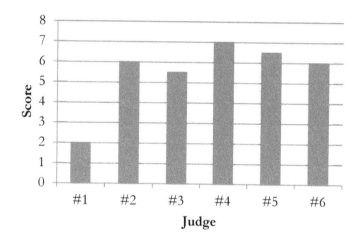

To calculate the diver's final score, the highest score and the lowest score are discarded and then the mean is found for the remaining four scores. What was the final score for this dive?

   (A) 5.5
   (B) 6.0
   (C) 6.5
   (D) 7.0

CONTINUE TO THE NEXT PAGE

11. What is the value of $6 + 5 \times 4 - 8 \div 2$?

   (A) 18
   (B) 20
   (C) 22
   (D) 24

12. The first five terms of a sequence are shown below.

   $$5, 10, 15, 20, 25$$

   Which expression could be used to find the nth term in this sequence?

   (A) $n + 5$
   (B) $2n - 5$
   (C) $5n$
   (D) $10n - 5$

13. A figure is created by joining two semi-circles to a rectangle, as shown below. The dimensions of the rectangle are 6 cm by 9 cm.

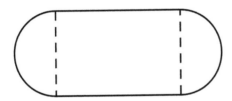

   What is the perimeter of the figure?

   (A) $18 + 6\pi$
   (B) $18 + 12\pi$
   (C) $30 + 6\pi$
   (D) $30 + 12\pi$

CONTINUE TO THE NEXT PAGE

14. Use the table below to answer the question.

$$2^1 = 2$$
$$2^2 = 4$$
$$2^3 = 8$$
$$2^4 = 16$$
$$2^5 = 32$$
$$2^6 = 64$$

What would be the units digit of 2^{18}?

(A) 2

(B) 4

(C) 6

(D) 8

15. The diagram below shows a circle inscribed inside a square. The side length of the square is 12 cm.

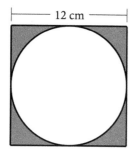

What is the area of the shaded region?

(A) $(48 - 6\pi)$ cm²

(B) $(48 - 12\pi)$ cm²

(C) $(144 - 12\pi)$ cm²

(D) $(144 - 36\pi)$ cm²

CONTINUE TO THE NEXT PAGE

16. The box-and-whisker plot below represents the number of students absent from a school each day in the month of January.

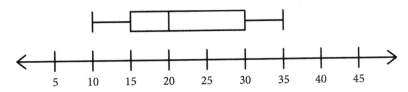

    What is the range of this data?

    (A) 20
    (B) 25
    (C) 30
    (D) 35

17. The table below shows a pattern.

Input	Output
1	0
2	3
3	6
•	•
•	•
•	•
n	q

    If the pattern shown above continues, then $q =$

    (A) $3(n - 1)$
    (B) $3n - 1$
    (C) $2n$
    (D) $2(n - 1)$

18. Darnell had scores of 90, 88, and 84 on his first three tests. What score must he receive on his fourth test to achieve a mean score of 90 on all four tests?

    (A) 90
    (B) 93
    (C) 96
    (D) 98

CONTINUE TO THE NEXT PAGE

19. If a number is a multiple of both 4 and 6, what other number must it also be a multiple of?

   (A) 8
   (B) 12
   (C) 18
   (D) 24

20. The square of a number is equal to six less than five times that number. Which equation could be used to solve for the number?

   (A) $x^2 = 6 - 5x$
   (B) $x^2 = 5x - 6$
   (C) $x^2 - 6 = 5x$
   (D) $x^2 + 6 = -5x$

21. A varies inversely with the square of B. If B is doubled, then the value of A will be

   (A) one-fourth of its original value
   (B) halved
   (C) doubled
   (D) quadrupled

22. The length of a rectangle was increased by 10% and the width was decreased by 20%. The area of this new rectangle is what percent of the area of the original rectangle?

   (A) 88%
   (B) 90%
   (C) 100%
   (D) 110%

CONTINUE TO THE NEXT PAGE

23. The graph below shows the distances of four students from their school.

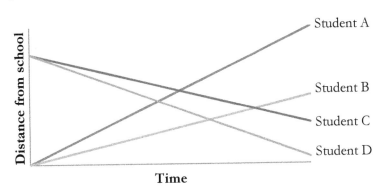

Which student is walking toward the school at the greatest rate?

(A) Student A

(B) Student B

(C) Student C

(D) Student D

24. The height of the cone shown below is half of its diameter. The formula used to find the volume of a cone is $V = \frac{1}{3}\pi r^2 h$, where r is the radius of the cone and h is the height of the cone.

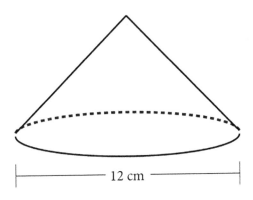

12 cm

If the diameter of the cone is 12 cm, then what is its volume, in cm³?

(A) 72π

(B) 144π

(C) 216π

(D) $1,440\pi$

CONTINUE TO THE NEXT PAGE

25. A number line is shown below.

Which point represents $-2\frac{3}{4}$?

(A) A

(B) B

(C) C

(D) D

26. The table below shows the results of a survey of 90 children. Each student was asked about his or her favorite summertime activity.

Activity	Number of Children
Camping	30
Swimming	25
Baseball games	18
Other	17

If a circle graph was made using this data, what would be the central angle of the section representing swimming?

(A) 25°

(B) 75°

(C) 100°

(D) 125°

27. If $\frac{r}{5} = \frac{r}{6}$, then what is the value of r?

(A) $\frac{6}{5}$

(B) 1

(C) $\frac{5}{6}$

(D) 0

CONTINUE TO THE NEXT PAGE

28. The graph of a line is shown below.

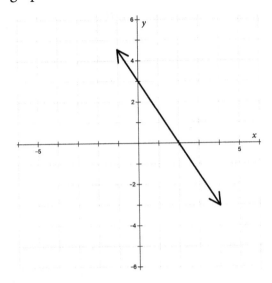

What is the slope of this line?

(A) $-\dfrac{3}{2}$

(B) $-\dfrac{2}{3}$

(C) $\dfrac{2}{3}$

(D) $\dfrac{3}{2}$

29. If $\dfrac{6x-2y}{2} = 3(x + my)$, what is the value of m?

(A) $-\dfrac{1}{3}$

(B) $\dfrac{1}{3}$

(C) 3

(D) 6

CONTINUE TO THE NEXT PAGE

30. The price of a shirt is increased by 20%. A week later, this new price is then decreased by 30% for a sale. What percent of the original price is the sale price?

    (A) 84%

    (B) 90%

    (C) 92%

    (D) 100%

31. The stem and leaf plot below shows the scores on a history test.

6	8	8	9	9					
7	1	2	3	5	5	6	6	7	9
8	0	0	1	1	1	2	3	5	5	6	9
9	1	1	4	5	6	7	8	8	9

Which box-and-whisker plot accurately represents this data?

(A)

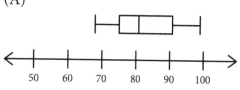

(B)

(C)

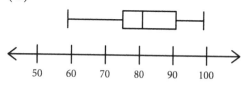

(D)

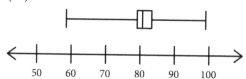

32. What are the possible values of x if $|x + 2| < 4$

    (A) $-6 < x < 2$

    (B) $-6 < x < 6$

    (C) $-2 < x < 2$

    (D) $2 < x < 6$

CONTINUE TO THE NEXT PAGE

33. Which graph shows the solution set for the inequality $32 \leq 3x < 54$?

(A)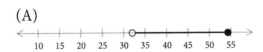

(B)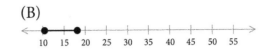

(C)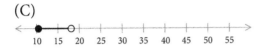

(D)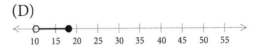

34. The box-and-whisker plot below shows the number of students at each school in a school district.

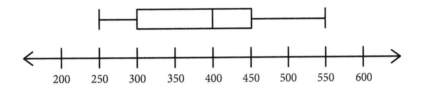

What is the range of this data?

(A) 250
(B) 300
(C) 400
(D) 550

35. What is the value of the expression $\sqrt{9 + 16}$?

(A) 5
(B) 6
(C) 7
(D) 9

36. A box of crackers is supposed to contain 60 crackers. However, the actual number of crackers is allowed to be within 3 of this number. Which equation represents the number of crackers (c) allowed in each box?

(A) $|c - 3| = 60$
(B) $|c - 3| \leq 60$
(C) $|c - 60| \leq 3$
(D) $|c - 60| \geq 3$

CONTINUE TO THE NEXT PAGE

37. A coin is flipped three times. The possible outcomes of landing on heads (H) and tails (T) are shown in the table below.

TTT	HHH
THT	HHT
TTH	HTT
THH	HTH

What is the probability that exactly two of the tosses will land on heads?

(A) $\dfrac{1}{8}$

(B) $\dfrac{1}{4}$

(C) $\dfrac{3}{8}$

(D) $\dfrac{1}{2}$

38. What is the most reasonable unit for measuring the height of a school?

(A) millimeters

(B) centimeters

(C) meters

(D) kilometers

CONTINUE TO THE NEXT PAGE

39. The graph of line m is shown below.

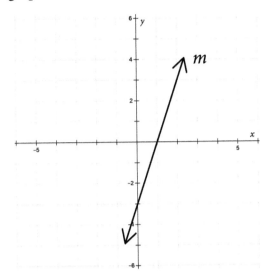

Line p (not shown) is perpendicular to line m. What is the slope of line p?

(A) -3

(B) $-\dfrac{1}{3}$

(C) $\dfrac{1}{3}$

(D) 3

40. Gayle is rolling two six-sided cubes. The sides of each cube are labeled 1-6. What is the probability that the first roll results in an even number and the second roll results in a 1 or 3?

(A) $\dfrac{1}{6}$

(B) $\dfrac{1}{3}$

(C) $\dfrac{1}{2}$

(D) $\dfrac{5}{6}$

CONTINUE TO THE NEXT PAGE

41. What is the solution set for $8 < -3x + 2 < 17$?

    (A) $2 < x < 5$

    (B) $x > 2,\ x < 5$

    (C) $-5 < x < -2$

    (D) $x < -5,\ x > -2$

42. What is the most reasonable unit for measuring the mass of a pencil?

    (A) milligrams

    (B) grams

    (C) kilograms

    (D) tons

43. Which expression does NOT represent a rational number?

    (A) $\sqrt{\dfrac{4}{2}}$

    (B) $\sqrt{\dfrac{9}{4}}$

    (C) $\dfrac{\sqrt{36}}{5}$

    (D) $\dfrac{\sqrt{28}}{\sqrt{7}}$

44. Five people are running a race. If every person finishes the race at a different time, in how many different orders could they finish?

    (A) 5

    (B) 30

    (C) 60

    (D) 120

CONTINUE TO THE NEXT PAGE

45. There are six possible toppings for a pizza. If Nick is going to choose three different toppings for his pizza, how many combinations are possible for those three toppings?

    (A) 10
    (B) 20
    (C) 30
    (D) 90

46. Which graph represents $x \geq 4$ or $x < 1$?

    (A)
    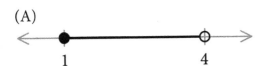
    1   4

    (B)
    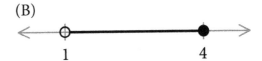
    1   4

    (C)

    1   4

    (D)

    1   4

47. Which graph represents the solution set for $2 < -2x + 2 < 10$?

    (A)

    (B)

    (C)

    (D)

STOP

IF YOU HAVE TIME LEFT YOU MAY CHECK YOUR ANSWERS IN THIS SECTION ONLY

Essay

You will be given 30 minutes to plan and write an essay. The topic is printed on the next page. *Make sure that you write about this topic. Do NOT choose another topic.*

This essay gives you the chance to show your thinking and how well you can express your ideas. Do not worry about filling all of the space provided. The quality is more important than how much you write. You should write more than a brief paragraph, though.

A copy of this essay will be sent to the schools that you apply to. Make sure that you only write in the appropriate area on the answer sheet. Please print so that the admissions officers can understand what you wrote.

On the next page is the topic sheet. There is room on this sheet to make notes and collect your thoughts. The final essay should be written on the two lined sheets provided in the answer sheet, however. Make sure that you copy your topic at the top of the first lined page. Write only in blue or black ink.

Answer sheets are found near the beginning of this book.

REMINDER: Please remember to write the topic on the top of the first lined page in your answer sheet.

> What person from history do you most admire?
> Why do you admire this person?

- Write only about this topic
- Only the lined sheets will be sent to schools
- Use only blue or black ink

Notes

_____

_____

_____

_____

_____

_____

_____

_____

_____

_____

_____

_____

_____

_____

_____

_____

_____

Answers

Practice Test 1 Answers

Practice Test 1 – Verbal Reasoning Answers

Correct answer	Your answer	Put a checkmark here if you answered the question correctly
1. C		
2. D		
3. B		
4. A		
5. B		
6. C		
7. D		
8. A		
9. A		
10. D		
11. B		
12. C		
13. C		
14. D		
15. A		
16. B		
17. A		
18. D		
19. C		
20. A		
21. C		.
22. D		

23. D		
24. B		
25. C		
26. D		
27. C		
28. A		
29. B		
30. D		
31. C		
32. A		
33. C		
34. B		
35. D		
36. C		
37. B		
38. A		
39. D		
40. A		
Total questions answered correctly: _____		

Practice Test 1 – Quantitative Reasoning Answers

Correct answer	Your answer	Put a checkmark here if you answered the question correctly
1. C		
2. B		
3. D		
4. A		
5. C		
6. C		
7. D		
8. A		
9. B		
10. C		
11. D		
12. B		
13. D		
14. D		
15. D		
16. B		
17. D		
18. C		
19. A		
20. A		
21. C		
22. C		
23. B		
24. D		
25. B		

26. B		
27. B		
28. C		
29. D		
30. D		
31. A		
32. D		
33. A		
34. D		
35. C		
36. A		
37. A		
Total questions answered correctly: _____		

Practice Test 1 – Reading Comprehension Answers

Correct answer	Your answer	Put a checkmark here if you answered the question correctly
1. B		
2. A		
3. D		
4. C		
5. B		
6. D		
7. A		
8. B		
9. A		
10. D		
11. C		
12. D		
13. A		
14. D		
15. B		
16. B		
17. C		
18. A		
19. B		
20. C		
21. D		
22. A		
23. B		
24. A		
25. A		

26. D		
27. B		
28. C		
29. B		
30. D		
31. B		
32. D		
33. A		
34. C		
35. C		
36. A		
Total questions answered correctly: _____		

Practice Test 1 – Mathematics Achievement Answers

Correct answer	Your answer	Put a checkmark here if you answered the question correctly
1. B		
2. A		
3. C		
4. A		
5. B		
6. A		
7. C		
8. C		
9. C		
10. D		
11. D		
12. D		
13. D		
14. C		
15. B		
16. B		
17. D		
18. B		
19. A		
20. C		
21. C		
22. C		
23. D		
24. B		
25. C		

26. D		
27. C		
28. D		
29. D		
30. D		
31. B		
32. C		
33. B		
34. C		
35. C		
36. D		
37. C		
38. B		
39. B		
40. A		
41. D		
42. C		
43. D		
44. B		
45. D		
46. C		
47. D		
Total questions answered correctly: _____		

Practice Test 2 Answers

Practice Test 2 – Verbal Reasoning Answers

Correct answer	Your answer	Put a checkmark here if you answered the question correctly
1. A		
2. C		
3. B		
4. A		
5. D		
6. C		
7. B		
8. A		
9. C		
10. D		
11. D		
12. B		
13. A		
14. B		
15. C		
16. A		
17. B		
18. A		
19. D		
20. D		
21. A		
22. B		

23. A		
24. C		
25. D		
26. A		
27. B		
28. A		
29. B		
30. C		
31. D		
32. D		
33. B		
34. A		
35. D		
36. B		
37. D		
38. C		
39. D		
40. A		

Total questions answered correctly: _____

Practice Test 2 – Quantitative Reasoning Answers

Correct answer	Your answer	Put a checkmark here if you answered the question correctly
1. A		
2. C		
3. C		
4. D		
5. B		
6. D		
7. C		
8. C		
9. C		
10. A		
11. B		
12. B		
13. C		
14. D		
15. D		
16. A		
17. D		
18. A		
19. D		
20. A		
21. A		
22. B		
23. A		
24. D		
25. B		

26. C		
27. B		
28. C		
29. C		
30. D		
31. C		
32. A		
33. A		
34. B		
35. D		
36. C		
37. C		
Total questions answered correctly: _____		

Practice Test 2 – Reading Comprehension Answers

Correct answer	Your answer	Put a checkmark here if you answered the question correctly
1. B		
2. D		
3. A		
4. C		
5. D		
6. C		
7. B		
8. A		
9. A		
10. D		
11. C		
12. C		
13. D		
14. B		
15. C		
16. D		
17. A		
18. B		
19. C		
20. B		
21. A		
22. D		
23. B		
24. A		
25. D		

26. B		
27. C		
28. A		
29. B		
30. D		
31. C		
32. B		
33. A		
34. C		
35. B		
36. A		

Total questions answered correctly: _____

Practice Test 2 – Mathematics Achievement Answers

Correct answer	Your answer	Put a checkmark here if you answered the question correctly
1. C		
2. D		
3. D		
4. D		
5. A		
6. B		
7. A		
8. C		
9. B		
10. B		
11. C		
12. C		
13. A		
14. B		
15. D		
16. B		
17. A		
18. D		
19. B		
20. B		
21. A		
22. A		
23. D		
24. A		
25. A		

26. C		
27. D		
28. A		
29. A		
30. A		
31. A		
32. A		
33. C		
34. B		
35. A		
36. C		
37. C		
38. C		
39. B		
40. A		
41. C		
42. B		
43. A		
44. D		
45. B		
46. D		
47. B		
Total questions answered correctly: _____		

Interpreting Your Scores

On the ISEE, your raw score is the number of questions that you answered correctly on each section. Nothing is subtracted for the questions that you answered incorrectly.

Your raw score is then converted into a scaled score. This scaled score is then converted into a percentile score. Remember that it is the percentile score that schools are looking at. Your percentile score compares you just to other students in your grade.

Below is a series of charts, one for each section of the test. The charts provide a very rough conversion between your raw score on each section and a percentile score.

> PLEASE NOTE – The purpose of these charts is to illustrate how the scoring works, not to give you an accurate percentile score. You will need to complete the official practice test in *What to Expect on the ISEE*, available for download from ERB at www.erblearn.org, in order to get a more accurate percentile score.

Upper Level – Verbal Reasoning

Approximate Raw Scores Needed to Achieve Percentiles

	25th	50th	75th
Applicants to Grade 9	16-17	21-22	27-28
Applicants to Grade 10	17-18	23-24	29-30
Applicants to Grade 11	18-19	24-25	30-31
Applicants to Grade 12	17-18	22-23	29-30

Upper Level – Quantitative Reasoning

Approximate Raw Scores Needed to Achieve Percentiles

	25th	50th	75th
Applicants to Grade 9	15-16	19-20	23-24
Applicants to Grade 10	15-16	20-21	25-26
Applicants to Grade 11	16-17	21-22	27-28
Applicants to Grade 12	17-18	21-22	25-26

Upper Level – Reading Comprehension

Approximate Raw Scores Needed to Achieve Percentiles

	25th	50th	75th
Applicants to Grade 9	17-18	21-22	27-28
Applicants to Grade 10	18-19	23-24	28-29
Applicants to Grade 11	18-19	24-25	29-30
Applicants to Grade 12	16-17	18-19	27-28

Upper Level – Mathematics Achievement

Approximate Raw Scores Needed to Achieve Percentiles

	25th	50th	75th
Applicants to Grade 9	19-20	24-25	29-30
Applicants to Grade 10	20-21	26-27	32-33
Applicants to Grade 11	22-23	28-29	34-35
Applicants to Grade 12	22-23	27-28	33-34